Lyke Wake Walk
and the Lyke Wake Way

Forty Miles across the North York Moors in
24 hours or 50 miles in as long as you like!

With in addition the Shepherd's Round,
the Monks' Trod and the Rail Trail
thrown in for good measure

by
Bill Cowley

Dalesman Books
1988

The Dalesman Publishing Company Ltd.,
Clapham, via Lancaster, LA2 8EB

First Published 1959
Eleventh Edition 1988

ISBN: 0 85206 959 6

Dedicated to all the friends who have walked with me over the years.

Printed by Smiths of Bradford, Bradford, West Yorkshire

Contents

Maps on pages 20 - 23 and 62 - 63 by Jean Cowley.
Map on page 11 by A.E.F. Wright.

Cleveland Lyke Wake Dirge

Richard Blakeborough's version with slight amendments and revised spelling.

> This yah neet, this yah neet,
>> Ivvery neet an all,
> Fire an fleet an cannle leet,
>> An Christ tak up thy saul.

> When thoo fra hence away art passed,
>> Ivvery neet an all,
> Ti Whinny Moor thoo cums at last,
>> An Christ tak up thy saul.

> If ivver thoo gav owther hosen or shoon,
>> Ivvery neet an all,
> Clap thee doon, an put em on,
>> An Christ tak up thy saul.

> Bud if hosen an shoon thoo nivver gav neean,
>> Ivvery neet an all,
> T'whinnies'll prick thee sair ti t'beean,
>> An Christ tak up thy saul.

> Fra Whinny Moor when thoo art passed,
>> Ivvery neet an all,
> Ti t' Brig o Dreead thoo cums at last,
>> An Christ tak up thy saul.

> If ivver thoo gav o thy siller an gowd,
>> Ivvery neet an all,
> On t'Brig o Dreead thoo'll finnd foothod,
>> An Christ tak up thy saul.

> Bud if siller an gowd thoo nivver gav neean,
>> Ivvery neet an all,
> Thoo'll doon, doon tummle towards Hell fleeam,
>> An Christ tak up thy saul.

> Fra t' Brig o Dreead when thoo art passed,
>> Ivvery neet an all,
> Ti t'fleeams o Hell thoo cums at last,
>> An Christ tak up thy saul.

> If ivver thoo gav owther bite or sup,
>> Ivvery neet an all,
> T' fleeams'll nivver catch thee up,
>> An Christ tak up thy saul.

> Bud if bite or sup thoo niver gave neean,
>> Ivvery neet an all,
> T' fleeams'll bon thee sair ti' t'beean,
>> An Christ tak up thy saul.

Fleet – sparks, embers; **yah** – one; **beean** – bone; **bon** – burn.

Origins of the Lyke Wake Walk

THE Lyke Wake Walk began with an article in *The Dalesman* for August 1955. I then had an interest in Glaisdale Head Farm, with rights of turbary under the Danby Manor Court Leet. It was whilst digging peat on Cockheads (now sadly all burnt out by the disastrous fire of 1976) that I thought of the twenty miles of heather between there and my main farm at Ravenscar, dimly seen to the east. The challenge to walk this in twenty four hours was soon taken up and the first crossing occurred on October 1st, 1955. Struggling through deep heather on Wheeldale Moor at 3.00 a.m. with storm threatening we cheered each other on by reciting the Lyke Wake Dirge. This mediaeval dirge was mentioned by John Aubrey in 1686 as being sung at funerals 'by the vulgar people in Yorkshire'. Appropriately it suggests that everyone, after death, has to make a journey over a wide and difficult moor. If you've done good deeds during your life – given away socks and shoes, silver and gold, food and drink – aid will be given you and you'll get across safely, to Paradise or Ravenscar, whichever you happen to be making for. But if not, then you'll sink into Hell flames or into the Rosedale bog!

'Wake' is the watching over a corpse, and 'lyke' is the corpse itself – as in the 'lych' gate of a church where the coffin was rested. Canon Atkinson of Danby believed that 'fleet' (in 'Fire an fleet an cannle leet') was a variant of 'flet', a Cleveland term for live coals or embers, some of which in his early days in Danby (1840s) would still be thrown into the open grave.

The ideas in the dirge go back to very early folk-lore – perhaps even to the Bronze Age people who burned and buried their dead on the high points of our moors, where their grave mounds or 'howes' are now our guiding marks right across the moors. Apart from these burials, there is no suggestion that corpses were ever carried over the length of the Lyke Wake Walk, though many who walk it have felt like corpses on arrival. However, the coffin and the candle are incorporated in the Lyke Wake Club badge and the Club's main business meeting is at the Candlemas Wake in February.

When You are on the Moors

THE art of moorland walking is always to look well ahead and pick a route that will take advantage of sheep tracks, short heather, and burnt patches of "swiddens". On a well-cared-for moor, the heather is never allowed to grow too long but patches are burned in rotation, young heather shoots being a favourite food of both grouse and sheep.

It is better to detour a little than to plough through deep heather on a compass course, and it will cause far less disturbance to grouse in the nesting season. Parties should walk in single file and be as. quiet as possible. Spreading out and shouting, particularly at night, with lights, can scare sheep into running to their deaths in a bog. A solemn silence should always prevail on the Lyke Wake Walk.

Give shooting parties a very wide berth in your own interest as well as theirs. It is important always to be careful where you go and how you go, and to retain the friendship of all concerned. Please never leave litter of any kind unless it is well buried. A tin can lame a sheep, a bottle can start a fire.

Remember – this is a tough walk. In really bad winter conditions it can be impossible. Never tackle it unless fully trained and prepared. Don't be afraid to turn back. Never go on to Wheeldale or Fylingdale Moors alone if already exhausted. Think of others – and do not expect a welcome at any farm or inn at unreasonable hours.

In thick mist be careful on Carlton and Cringle Moors. Watch out for rock outcrops, and for high embankments along the old railway.

SEVEN POINTS OF SAFETY

The greatest danger on the North Yorkshire Moors lies in sudden changes of weather. You can have sunshine in the morning and hailstones in the afternoon. A light drizzle in the valley may be a blizzard on the moor-top. Therefore remember

1. Always take map and compass (and make sure you can use

them)

2. Carry a wind-proof anorak and spare warm clothing even in summer. Wear boots.
3. Pack a torch, a reserve of food, a small first-aid kit, and a *whistle* (which in emergency carries further and lasts longer than the human voice).
4. Always leave word of your route, and stick to it. Make sure *someone* knows where you have gone. Have a central phone number to report to if you give up, or inform the police so that time is not wasted looking for you.
5. A safe number for a party is five. If anyone is hurt two can stay with him and two go for help.
6. Study the map, and note the quickest and safest ways to get off the moors, and the nearest telephones.
7. If hopelessly lost at night, shelter in deep heather, out of the wind, eat some of your emergency food, and wait for daylight. Put all spare clothing on immediately you stop, *before* you begin to get cold. And stop *before* you are exhausted. In an emergency, inform the police as soon as possible.

ROUTE PLANNING

For a summer daylight crossing it is best to start at 4 a.m. after a night's sleep and walk straight through to finish by 10 p.m. For a party not too fit a good way is to start at 6 p.m., sleep at Clay Bank 10 p.m. to 4 a.m. and finish at 6 p.m. again. Keep a rough time schedule for each section. Restrict rest stops to 15 mins. or at most 30 mins. Leave some agreed sign at crossing points if you decide to go on before your support party arrives (e.g. an arrow of small stones indicating a note – *not* indiscriminate chalk marks, please). A good average time is 15 hours.

EQUIPMENT

Footwear – Walking shoes or gym shoes are not suitable for moorland walking. *Always* wear boots. these need not be expensive, but they must be strong and large enough to wear with *two* pairs of socks. Soft fell boots are best. In dry summer conditions basketball boots may be useful.

Clothing – Always wear (or carry) long trousers, preferably made of wool or cord. Jeans are most unsuitable as they retain little warmth and corduroys are difficult to dry. An anorak or wind-cheater is essential. This should be as windproof and as waterproof as possible, whilst avoiding condensation on the inside. Rubber materials are unsuitable.

A plastic mackintosh or a waterproof cover made from one of the new proofed nylon materials is the best protection against heavy rain. Carry spare emergency clothing; if the weather should deteriorate it will save you a lot of discomfort and hardship.

HEATHER BIVOUACS

Even in winter a night on the moors need not be disastrous. If near a valley, go down into it to the first bracken, and make a deep nest of bracken and heather, pulling plenty on top of you. On the moor itself find a patch of deep heather and a sheltered hollow. Use loose stones to build a windbreak. Pull enough heather to make a bed below and a blanket on top.

NOTE:

Some of this information may not seem necessary now on the Classic Route of the Lyke Wake Walk. But anyone who can read a map and use a compass will enjoy the challenge of pathfinding elsewhere on the moors. Just remember that a small party of two or three, moving quietly and unobtrusively, can travel without complaint where larger parties can meet difficulties and objections. Care and courtesy are always worthwhile.

There are now many 'named' walks on these moors – the Bilsdale Circuit, the Rosedale Circuit and a dozen more. But every walker, with a little experience, should be able to study a map and plan his own walk. He may not get a badge for it, but he will get much more satisfaction. The challenge and triumph of finding the right line across a trackless moor must compare with that of the early navigators making a correct landfall across a wide ocean.

Lyke Wake Walk 1988

WHEN the Lyke Wake Walk was started in 1955, and for many years thereafter, the challenge was not just distance but also moorcraft and pathfinding. Apart from Scugdale and the Wheeldale Youth Hostel, there was then no human habitation on or near the route, and most of the route was by narrow sheep track or almost trackless heather. There were unexploded shells on Fylingdales – in the first few years firing was still to be heard from Jugger Howe and we tended to keep well south of Jugger Howe Beck. One party stumbled over a notice which said 'Mines'. But there was no Early Warning Station, no Bilsdale Mast, no fire-breaks over any moors, no forestry, no gliders. Since then that complete wildness has been lost; 30,000 acres of moor have gone to forestry, and some 11,000 acres to farming. That is 25% of the original moorland area. I am not opposed to forestry. I would even like to see more of it in bracken-infested valleys, as in Wheeldale Gill. But there is no joy in walking through miles of pine and spruce with no view but trees. We cannot afford to lose any more heather moor to forestry. Still less can we afford to lose it to agriculture. The overwhelming claim to the little wild country that is now left in England must be for recreation. Again, there are many old intakes, and bracken infested areas, which could reasonably be reclaimed for farming. But it is quite unreasonable that public money should be spent in grants for reclamation of heather moor, when to reclaim it is manifestly against the general public's interest. All who love the moors should join in resisting any further encroachment upon them.

In 1988 the heather moors of North-East Yorkshire are in more danger than they have ever been. The 'heather economy' has long been based on grouse shooting and sheep rearing. The costs of both have increased, to a greater extent than the returns. There are fewer keepers, and fewer shepherds. Without an adequate labour force heather does not get regularly burnt off to encourage young growth. Deep old heather is difficult to walk through and is a real fire risk. An uncontrolled moor fire can devastate a large area as in 1976 and render it useless for either sheep or grouse. The danger is that then forestry or agricultural improvement will be difficult to withstand. Therefore always have close regard to any damage you may be causing to land, game and stock. Above all never spread out, never smoke in heather, make as little noise as possible, and never ever leave tins and bottles on the moor. Even if you do not approve of shooting remember that the continuance of well-kept heather moor depends on the landowner getting good rents for his grouse shooting.

At the same time as these encroachments, the number of walkers using the moors has gone on increasing. The Lyke Wake route is now a well-trodden path from start to finish, in some places too well and too widely trodden. It is almost impossible to lose the way in ordinary conditions, though in darkness or fog some people still manage to do so. Gone however (one hopes) are the days when a party could walk steadily for five hours and then find themselves only three miles from the starting point.

Damage done by walkers to the moors is very small in comparison with that done by other agencies and by natural erosion. Walkers however must do all they can to limit any damage they may cause. They can do this in several ways.

1. Keep parties small. Ten should be a maximum. Parties of three or four hundred, with large buses blocking the support roads, are really ridiculous and destroy the basic idea of this walk. Large parties also tend to straggle and to spread out more, causing more damage. Large sponsored walks should turn their attention elsewhere, and some suggestions for this are made later.

2. Keep together, and keep to the same narrow track, walking no more than two abreast and preferably in single file. If this involves going through what seems the wettest part of the bog, go through it. You are going to get wet anyway. By treading out wide you are merely spreading the bog.

3. In training walks, avoid using the sections mentioned, particularly Loose Howe to Blue Man.

It must be remembered that though much of the Lyke Wake route lies along the old Cleveland boundary, which is itself often the dividing line between different estates, beyond Rosedale very little of it is a definitive right-of-way though it may now be a de-facto one. It is hoped that some sort of linear access agreement will eventually be made, and that it will be possible with the help of the

10

Countryside Commission, the National Park, and the Yorkshire and Humberside Council for Sport and Recreation, to consolidate or repair the worst sections of the route, and to maintain it. For some this will lessen still further the challenge of the route but with the numbers involved there is no alternative.

The Lyke Wake Walk has sometimes been criticised for attracting so many for the first time to the beauty of the high moors and the fascination of crossing them by day and by night, in all weathers. A minority, like a minority of motorists, misbehave. Most who come for the challenge become real lovers of the moors, of which the Lyke Wake Club exhorts all its members to take proper care. Any negative attitude to this type of walk is regrettable. It is foolish to complain of the younger generation and yet limit in any way the few opportunities for adventure and exploration in wild places that still exist. That thousands of people every year are prepared to complete the arduous 40 miles of the Lyke Wake Walk is something to be proud of. These and many more will come to this and other 'open country' walks whatever difficulties are placed in their way. But with goodwill on all sides the good far outweighs the harm.

NUMBERS

Crossings reported rose from 176 in the first three years 1955-58 to 10,000 in 1979 since when there has been a steady decrease to about 3,000 a year, the total reported being now 135,000. About 6% are by women, 12% are second or later crossings and 12% are East to West.

THE LOCATION

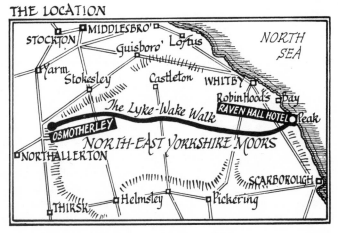

The First Crossing

WE knew it would be a tough test – a minor Everest of our own making. We had all lived with maps in hand or mind for days, weighing alternative routes. Now came the final choice – and the weather was perfect.

We took the alum miner's track round the face of Carlton Moor, Cringle Moor and Cold Moor, with the Cleveland Plain below stretching away to the Pennines by Cross Fell, or across smoky Tees-side to the Durham hills. Four of us reached Clay Bank Top in 2½ hours, glad of the mobile bar that awaited us!

We reached the high point of Botton Head (1,489 ft.) right on schedule at 3.30 p.m. Now we were deep in the moors and deep in heather. All our concentration was required to find the easiest and the shortest way through, a Bronze Age mound or a leaning stone our guide, to the Smugglers' Trod, its stone flags now heaved crazily about by heather roots. Darkness was just closing in on us as we saw the lights and tents of our bivouac round the ruined inn of Hamer. The Cleveland Lyke Wake Dirge came to our minds:

> This yah neet, this yah neet,
> Ivvery neet an' all,
> Fire an' fleet an' cannle leet,
> An' Christ tak up thy saul.

We gave a great shout and rushed down through the heather. We had covered 21 miles in seven hours and had earned a rest. Few of us got much sleep. The worst part still lay ahead. The real testing time of this walk started at 3.30 a.m. Before us was the wild stretch of Wheeldale Moor, with never a track across it. Just four miles of knee-deep heather till we reached the Roman highway at the other side.

The moon was veiled by clouds. The light and the contours were deceitful. We felt rather than saw the sudden drop into Wheeldale Gill, our guide to the left. To the right was only the cold night wind on our cheeks. Startled grouse kept exploding from the heather at our feet and grumbling away into the darkness. Shallow dips seemed like deep valleys, and sometimes we fell full length in an unseen hole.

> 'Twere a dree neet, a dree neet, ower Whinny Moor ti trake,
> Wi' shoonless feet, ower flinty steeans, thruff monny a thorny brake;
> A dree neet, a dree neet, wi' nowt neeaways ti mark
> T'gainest trod ti t'Brig o' Dreead, a lane lost sowl i' t' dark.

We kept checking our course by compass, slightly south of east. One solitary light in Goathland gave us another check, then suddenly an intake wall loomed ahead by the Stape road. Beyond was Wade's Causeway and the steep track down to a dark and silent Wheeldale Lodge. At 5.30 a.m. we were sitting on the stepping stones chewing chocolate, the wide stream a subdued silver between rustling trees. There was another hard climb through rocks and bracken on to Howl Moor. Dawn broke slowly as we approached the railway cutting at Ellerbeck. We crossed by Fen House, over Tom Cross Rigg to the Whitby road. A rest and a cold breakfast, and we set off along the Salt track for Lilla Howe.

It was 10 a.m. as we crossed the Scarborough road near Helwath Bridge and knew we were well inside the time. Even so, the last rough patches of heather over Pye Rigg Howe were a trial, and it was with weary limbs and sore heels, but glad hearts, that we tramped into Ravenscar at last down the road from the old windmill. Blue sea and golden sands were just beginning to show through the mist as the sun gained strength, and the cliffs beyond the bay took shape as we celebrated our triumph with the Goulton Tankard and formed the Lyke Wake Club.

In the Lyke Wake Country

HE who would enjoy the Lyke Wake Walk, and other such walks, to the full, must know the country intimately – its geography, its geology and its history. The North Yorkshire Moors contain 600 square miles of wild moorlands and lovely valleys, many of them quite uninhabited. A lifetime is insufficient to know the whole area as it should be known. Here ancient superstitions, and an ancient language, lingered till very recently.

From the long fertile Vale of Pickering rise first the Tabular Hills of Coralline Limestone, whose steep northern scarps, from Black Hambleton to Barns Cliff and Silpho, are always prominent in the Lyke Wake landscape to the south. 'North of the Tabular escarpment', writes Dr. Elgee, 'rolls a sea of heather-clad moor, one of the largest uncultivated tracts in England, the dominant feature of the district from time immemorial. Eight hundred years ago it was known as Blackamore. John of Hexham, writing in the days of Henry II, states that Rievaulx Abbey was situated "in solitudine Blackaumor". Leland speaks of the "very brows of Blakmore". Camden states that "among the mountains of Blackamore there is nothing remarkable, besides some rambling brooks and rapid torrents, which take up all the vallies hereabouts". Drayton's *Polyolbion* in 1622 mentioned "large-spread Blackimore."'

Geologically, the Tabular Hills are Middle Oolite and their conspicuous character is due to hard beds of Calcareous Grit and Coralline Oolite on top of 150 feet of Oxford Clay, itself above a band of Kelloway Rock. The high moors are Lower Oolite – Moor Grit and Fossiliferous Grit on top of thick beds of yellow Estuarine Sandstones, separated from the underlying Lias by that very variable band, the Dogger. Though the main Cleveland iron seams are in the Lias, the Rosedale seams were in the Oolite – in the Dogger – and there are also occasional small pockets of coal and limestone.

The Lias beds are the foundation of our moors and give them

much of their character – the steep northern scarp of the Cleveland Hills, and the deep narrow valleys. At the top of the Lias, just below the ferruginous band of Dogger, occur the alum shales, a hundred feet thick. In the 16th century the Chaloners of Guisborough brought home to Cleveland the method of alum extraction. Aluminium sulphate was produced by calcination from the alum shale, dissolved in water, a potassium salt added, and the alum precipitated as a fine powder. New and cheaper processes killed this industry in the middle of the last century.

Below the alum shales is the Jet Rock, a series of shales sometimes so bituminous that they ignite spontaneously, as on Boulby Cliff. Hence the red colour of some shale tips. Jet itself is of uncertain occurrence, and though plenty of jet ornaments are on sale in Whitby they are mostly of Spanish jet. Yet in 1872 jet working employed 1,500 persons and the value of the trade was £88,000. There is a Jeater Houses between Thirsk and Osmotherley, and a *Jet Miners' Inn* at Great Broughton. 'Striking a good seam' had a particular local application in Cleveland speech. Probably the last to be found and worked was by an aged jet miner in Rosedale, about 1885, near the Hamer road. Having no legal rights, he worked it at night, and succeeded in reaping the benefit of his experience and observation. Apart from iron, jet is the characteristic mineral of our moors. Nowhere else in England does it occur in such quantity or quality, and it has been known and used since Neolithic days. Pre-historic man, ancient Briton, Roman, Saxon, Dane, Viking and Norman have all admired and worn 'Whitby' jet.

The high moors crossed on the Lyke Wake Walk are of enormous antiquity, having been a land surface since the close of the Chalk Period, three to six million years ago. Tropical plants grew on them in the early stages and the petrified trunk of a large cycad tree was exposed in a sandstone quarry below Scarth Wood Moor towards the Sheepwash. There are one or two traces of Stone Age men just before or during lulls in the Great Ice Age, and the last survivors of these ancient hunters left pygmy-flints in moorland camps as at Cockheads, near Hamer, round 6000 B.C. 'Like stray shafts of sunshine', writes Dr. Elgee, 'their small imperishable flints illuminate the depths of gloomy avenues of time. They give us glimpses of skin-clad men spearing salmon in the Esk, or stalking deer over the melancholy moors – of women tending campfires on the heathery knolls whence craftsmen in the intervals of flint-chipping swept an eye over their hunting-grounds rolling to distant land and sea horizons.'

The stone-axe men of the Early Bronze Age who followed them on the limestone hills and elsewhere, and the long-barrow men still later (after 2000 B.C.), never inhabited the high moors, and I like to think the early hunters survived there. It was not until about 1000 B.C. that the mid-Bronze Age round-barrow people, who had come over from Denmark and the Rhinelands, began to inhabit the moors, driven to those inhospitable heights by other invaders from Central Europe, the Brigantes, a name probably meaning 'Mountain men'. About 400 B.C. from France came the Parisii who occupied the Wolds and drove the ancient urn people who remained there to join their relatives on the moors. When the Romans came to conquer the Brigantes and Parisii, descendants of the urn people were still clinging to the high moors, living on in the primitive fashion of their ancestors. With the coming of the Anglo-Saxons some Britons in their turn had to flee to the moors, which likewise must have long remained a British island in a Saxon sea, as many Celtic place names bear witness.

There was a new series of Scandinavian invasions, with the Danes in the ninth century, and then the Norwegians. Some came direct, and there were some from Ireland, through Cumberland, bringing with them Gaelic-Scandinavian place names. Farndale may be one. Barnscliffe, the cleft through which the waters of Bloody Beck, Jugger Howe Beck and Derwent find their way, is the Gaelic *bearna*, a cleft between two hills. It is probable that Norwegians re-populated parts of North Yorkshire after its harrying and devastation by William the Conqueror, and that immigrants were still coming in in the 12th century. Except for a few British names, the Scandinavian influence is paramount in our place names as in our dialect. The few Britons who remained on the high moors, whence the last of the aboriginals must by now have long since vanished, were probably not exterminated but just swamped by the Norwegians, who were attracted to the moors and the dales perhaps because of the resemblance to their native land.

The Romans left the high moors untouched save for Wade's Causeway. The Britons left a few names and some traces of Celtic fields near Commondale, Wardle Rigg, and Cloughton (south of Ravenscar). But the Bronze Age Round-barrow People or Urn Folk have left their monuments all over the moors. Their barrows or howes (O. N. *haugr*, a mound), and their standing stones, are our landmarks from one end of the Lyke Wake Walk to the other, though most have been given Norse names by later invaders. These people buried some of their dead unburned – the ordinary folk, perhaps – but the chiefs and leading members of the tribe were all cremated before burial, and the remains placed in urns under the barrows which were often sited on territorial boundaries (as they still are). Dr. Elgee thought there might be 10,000 barrows of various sizes on the uplands of north-east Yorkshire. The idea of cremation was probably to prevent the ghosts of the dead from returning to trouble the living, and some of this superstition lingered on in the dales until modern times in the throwing of charcoal into graves. It is perhaps echoed in the Lyke Wake Dirge – 'Fire an' fleet an' cannle leet'.

Sometimes these burials are also marked by stone circles like the one on the ridge between Bilsdale and Tripsdale, the Bridestones. Other stone circles and standing stones are connected with ceremonial – perhaps sacrificial–rites, with sun-worship and worship of a mother-goddess (derisively named the Old Wife in later folk-lore). Whether always associated with fertility rites or not, many of the standing stones must have been useful then, as they are to us now, as landmarks and guide-posts, for no doubt the sea-roke often came down on Botton Head and Shunner Howe as it does today! Many of the howes and stones lie in long lines, as on the ridge south from Carlton Bank, and on between Ryedale and Bilsdale, or right across Fylingdales from the Bridestones above Grosmont to the barrow groups on Maw Rigg above Langdale. Still more remarkable, however, are certain well-marked settlement sites on Danby Rigg, Crown End above Baysdale, and in many other places where whole cemeteries of barrows, entrenchments, hollow cattle-tracks, hut-sites and the remains of small fields have been traced. One of these is at the beginning of the Lyke Wake Walk, near Scarth Nick, and one at the end, between Pye Rigg Howe and Peak.

Some of the urn folk's sites are those of farms inhabited to this day. They themselves had sheep and cattle and a primitive agriculture. Their pathways ran mostly along the ridges, north and south, but there is little doubt that they would use the high water-shed for east-west crossing, and that we tread often in their footsteps. 'Their ultimate fate', says Elgee, 'is shrouded in darkness. Somewhere, at some time, a woman's deft fingers moulded the last urn, the wind drifted the smoke of the last funeral pyre over the moors, and the last cairn was piled over the dead., We who walk the high moors now cannot but be conscious everywhere of these long-vanished people.

The Lyke Wake, Mile by Mile

THE official starting point of the Lyke Wake Walk for all general purposes is the Lyke Wake Walk Stone on a little mound opposite the first car-park at the eastern end of the Osmotherley (Cod Beck) Reservoir. This is directly under the original starting point, the Triangulation pillar on Scarth Wood Moor near the TV Booster station (and the site of an Elizabethan warning beacon). Purists may like to go up to the pillar by an easy and obvious track but must not climb any stone walls. (Official records must be timed from the Triangulation Pillar to the bar of the Raven Hall Hotel). In order to lessen the chance of damage and disturbance others may go direct from the stone to Scarth Nick, and finish at the Beacon above Ravenscar.

The walk may be done either way, of course, but the prevailing winds being south-westerly a west-east crossing is usually easier. When a strong east wind is blowing however, as often in the early spring, the reverse is true.

Scarth Wood Moor makes a fine start for a walk, with views over to the Pennines. The flat top of the steep northern scarp of Pen Hill in Wensleydale, 28 miles away, is usually visible. On clear days you may see Mickle Fell (43 miles away) or, to the south-west, Buckden Pike and Great Whernside (34 miles).

The moor itself is full of interest. Presented to the National Trust in 1935 by Major G. H. Peake, grandfather of the present Lord Ingleby, of Snilesworth Hall, it contains Bronze Age barrows, and some ancient walling. There are three geological faults, the biggest being along the line of Scarth Nick. During the Ice Age a glacier 1000ft thick dammed up a lake in Scugdale. Overflows eroded one channel over Scarth Wood Moor from Sheath's Cottage (ruins) towards the Sheepwash, and another between Near Moor and Far Moor down Holywell Gill into Crabdale Beck a mile above the Sheepwash. When the lake level dropped, these two channels were put out of action and the water poured through Scarth Nick. (Scarth comes from Old Norse *skarthi,* a notch or cleft. It was also the nickname for a hare-lipped man and is still a good North Yorkshire surname).

From the top of Scarth Wood Moor you look east along your route, the magnificent front line of the Cleveland Hills, curving slightly north. Half of them are concealed by the rugged bulk of Carlton Bank, topped by a glider station. But beyond that you might just see the top of Botton Head, eleven miles on in your journey.

It is possible to go south-east over Near Moor or up Crabdale Beck to the Swainby shooting hut, over Whorlton Moor to Cock Howe and down Trinit (or Trennet) to Chop Gate (then by Bilsdale Hall to Botton Head). But there are no definitive footpaths and the route is certainly not suitable for large parties. (For me, a large party is anything over five!) It is more or less the route described so breezily by A. J. Brown in *Tramping in Yorkshire (North and East) Part Eight – Chequers to Chop Gate.* Most people take the 'front line', with its incomparable views over the Cleveland Plain, a patchwork quilt of rich pasture and arable fields stretching away to industrial Teesside, bounded on the east by Roseberry Topping (Odinsberg of the Vikings), 1,052 ft, and Captain Cook's Monument on Easby Moor, 1,064ft. If each peak in the 'front line' is taken direct there will be 2000 ft of climbing to Clay Bank on the Stokesley-Helmsley road. This makes a distinct first section of ten miles (2½-3 hours) different from the rest of the walk and the finest of introductions to it.

A very good training walk is to do this section, climb up to Botton Head, then return via Bilsdale Hall, Chop Gate and Cock Howe. The 20 miles of tough and varied going are equivalent to half the Lyke Wake Walk. True, the distance from Scarth Wood Moor to Ravenscar is only 35 miles as the crow flies, but it will be 40 as you walk, and as one Army sergeant remarked, 'It wasn't crows that measured these miles, it was bloody vultures!' There are 40 miles of heather and bog between you and the sea. You will cross three main roads, and walk a mile of secondary road. It is still possible occasionally, on a weekday, to do the whole walk and never meet a soul; and even now apart from a cottage in Scugdale and the Wheeldale Youth Hostel, you will pass no human habitation.

The road through Scarth Nick is the old drovers' road across Black Hambleton and was certainly a road long before the Romans came. When the plains were mostly forest and marsh this was the main route from York and Malton to the crossing of the Tees at Yarm, and it was commonly used until the railway era.

19

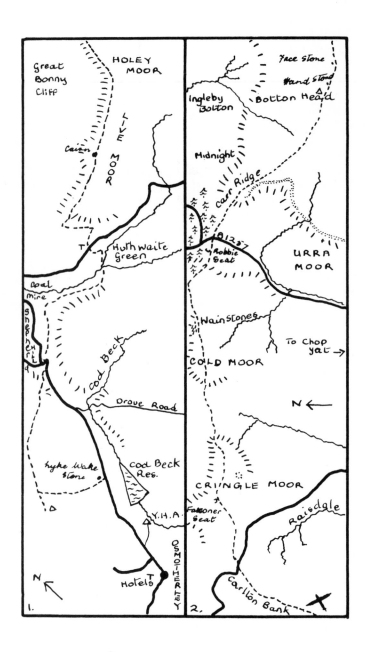

1.

Great
Bonny
Cliff

HOLEY
MOOR

L I V E
M O O R

Cairn

T

Huthwaite
Green

Coal
Mire

Shepherd
Hill

Cod Beck

Drove Road

Lyke Wake
Stone

Cod Beck
Res.

Y.H.A.

N

Hotels T

OSMOTHERLEY

2.

Face Stone

Hand Stone

Botton Head

Ingleby
Bolton

Midnight

Carr Ridge

1257

Robbie
Seat

URRA
MOOR

Nainstones

To Chop
Yat →

COLD MOOR

N ←

CRINGLE MOOR

Falconer
Seat

Raisdale

Carlton Bank

X

20

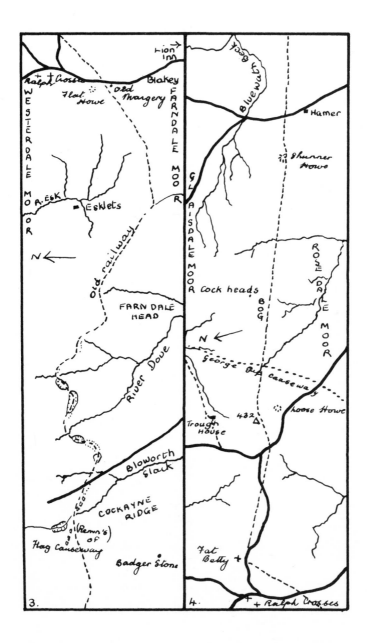

Map 3 (left panel):

Lion Inn →

Ralph Cross +
Blakey

Flat Howe
Old Margery

WESTERDALE MOOR

FARNDALE MOOR

R. Esk
Esklets

N ←

Old railway

FARNDALE HEAD

GLAISDALE MOOR

River Dove

Bloworth Slack

COCKAYNE RIDGE

(Remn's) of
Flag Causeway

Badger Stone

3.

Map 4 (right panel):

Bluewath Beck

Hamer

Shunner Howe

GLAISDALE MOOR

Cock heads

ROSEDALE MOOR

BOG

N ←

George Gap Causeway

432 △

Loose Howe

Trough House

Fat Betty +

+ Ralph Crosses

4.

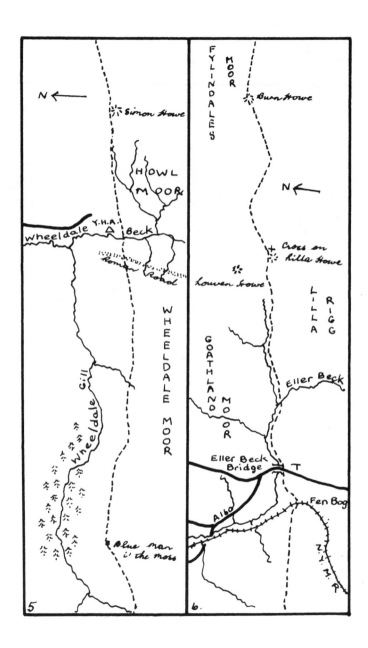

5

6.

22

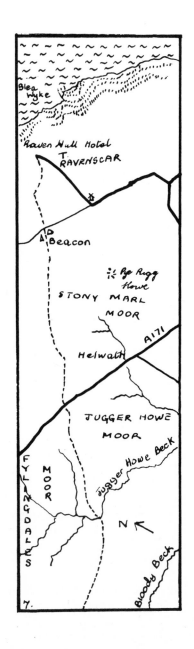

Blea
Wyke

Raven Hall Hotel
RAVENSCAR

Beacon

Rye Rigg
Howe

STONY MARL
MOOR

A171

Helwath

JUGGER HOWE
MOOR

F
Y
L
I
N
G
D
A
L
E
S

MOOR

Jugger Howe Beck

N

Bloody Beck

7.

23

Cross the road just above the cattle grid, and you will see a finger post *Ravenscar 39 miles*. The path goes through Coalmire Plantation to a knoll of grey shale practically in line with a hedge and wall going straight up the nose of Live Moor beyond. The wall is your next objective. To reach it go down the shale slope to the 'Lime-kiln Road' which goes left to the gamekeeper's cottage at Shepherd's Hill.

Jink slightly left across this green lane and down a hedge when you will strike the footpath running from Shepherd's Hill to Harfa Bank. This is now well indicated. It keeps well above a duck-pond, but soon afterwards you take a small wooden gate on the left, slanting across a grass field to the ford below Hollin Hill. Please keep the gate shut. From here a metalled road goes up to Huthwaite or Heathwaite Green where there is a telephone box. Here a gate opens on to a track that leads past an old iron mine (new planting here). Fork left at the second hedge towards some shale tips.

Above the shale tips you will find the long wall and steep climb up 'Knolls End' on to Live Moor. I have been told that the rather grassy moor beyond, Live Moor, used to provide common grazing for the donkeys which many Swainby villagers employed carrying coal and similar goods in the last century.

Some walkers, after struggling through Scugdale and up this steep knoll, have complained that 'Live' Moor is scarcely an appropriate name. But from here all is plain sailing, along the main watershed. All the springs and sikes to the right eventually flow to the Humber, those on the left to the Tees. On Live Moor, as on Whorlton Near Moor, are traces of ancient enclosures or field systems, and the main cairn is a 'hill fort'.

Looking north from Live Moor you see the prominent rounded outlier, Whorl Hill, beyond which lie the lands of Goulton Grange and Potto Hill, 'Whorl' is from Old Norse *hvirfill*, a rounded hill top. Between Whorl Hill and Swainby lie old Whorlton church and the 11th century motte and bailey castle of Whorlton, stronghold of Nicholas de Meynell, a famous Lyke Wake walker in his time, poaching the King's deer anywhere between here and Pickering. East of Whorl Hill lies Faceby, an interesting example of a Scandinavian nickname becoming a place name. It means, in fact, 'Fatty's farm'.

Below Holey Moor, Little Bonny Cliff and Great Bonny Cliff are fenced in by the Forestry Commission, but beyond them you will see the line of shale tips along the 900ft. contour which marks the old jet mines. Along the top of these goes an old jet miner's track which is sometimes useful when fog is thick on the tops themselves. It goes past John Quarry and Jackdaw Quarry to the old alum works on Carlton Bank. There is an inscription in Carlton churchyard to Tho. Sophle, Clarke to Capt. Christopr. Prissick's Allom Works, d. 1719. The route over the top of Carlton Bank is preferable, with long views back south down Thackdale (Snotterdale) into the upper part of Scugdale or over the long ridge between that dale and Raisdale to Green Howe and Cock Howe. Indeed at this point you are heading just slightly east of north, with the curve of the hills.

Go down the right-hand side of the alum workings to Carlton Bank top. Over the road is a grassy track leading up to Cringle Moor, locally 'Cringie'. By the roadside at a junction of parish boundaries, about the 975ft. level, may be found the Three Lords' Stone, the Lords at that time being Duncombe of Helmsley (now Feversham), Marwood of Busby Hall just below, and Ailesbury who at that time held Scugdale. I have seen a note by Major Fairfax-Blakeborough that 'On Easter Monday, 1905, a motor car driven by Mr Constantine ascended Carlton Bank to the amazement of everyone'. Now 'trial' motor cycles tear up and down the shale slopes shattering the peace of the moorlands above and the countryside below for miles. Much less objectionable is the quiet soaring, like great eagles, of the gliders that take off from Carlton Moor, though the Glider Club's wholesale levelling of the moor top is much to be regretted.

From Cringle there is a steep drop and a steep rise to Cold Moor (from which another fine ridge goes south to Chop Gate) followed by another drop and rise to Hasty Bank. You can if you wish bypass Cringle and Cold Moors by the jet miners' track along their northern face, but spurn the broad Forestry Commission track round Broughton Banks and strike up by the Wainstones (some fine short rock-climbs here) for the flat top of Hasty Bank. There is a good spring to the right – the Garfit side of the Wainstones. There are more rock-climbs further along the northern scarp of Hasty Bank, on Raven's Scar. Then you drop down to point 842 on Clay Bank Top ready for the first long spell and meal. This is a lovely spot, with the bluebell woods of Ingleby Bank on one side and Bilsdale stretching away on the other. The view north across (re-planted) woods is very fine, with the vale of Great Ayton and Kildale bounded on the far side by Easby Moor and Roseberry Topping. And if you think the smoky blur of Middlesbrough beyond a blot on the landscape, remember there too is romance. A century and a half ago there were only two farms on a mudflat by the Tees where now is an industrial jungle of blast furnaces and steel mills – all built from the very heart of the moors whereon we walk.

From Hagg's Gate (where the old road went down into Bilsdale via Holme Farm) you now have to climb to the highest point of the North Yorkshire Moors, Botton Head on Urra Moor, 1,489ft. Keep along the stone wall, boundary of the medieval Greenhowe deer park. You are on an ancient packhorse track used much at one time by smugglers. The track goes through a narrow cleft in the cliff and through a small gate on to the open moor of Carr Ridge, going still along a wall, and with a line of boundary stones to the right. Further to the right is a long line of entrenchments along the western edge of Urra Moor. Though attributed locally to Cromwell, they are at least medieval.

To the north is the rounded valley of Ingleby Botton -*botton* being a Scandinavian word meaning just this type of valley; hence Botton Head. On Bartholomew's map this is referred to as Burton Head – and no doubt the surveyor thought he was being clever, since of course the local pronunciation of Burton would be Bo'tton. A similar mistake occurs in Farndale, where 'Horn End' has been substituted for what is really Hon End – *hon* meaning a nab. Below, in the Botton, you may see Midnight (house) and Siberia (ruins). A visiting Methodist preacher at Ingleby got a shock when told that the meeting next Sunday would be at Midnight. The navvies who built the Rosedale railway lived at Siberia. Near a boundary stone on the 1,300 ft. contour is Maiden Spring, the source of the Seph which flows down between Cowkill Well and the Cheshire Stone and so down Bilsdale to the Rye. If you can select any part of this walk above others this is perhaps the finest, but one of the trickiest in bad conditions. This great moor, burned badly by a disastrous fire before the war and only just recovering 50 years later, has the most deceiving contours. To the right two shallow dips join to form the wild rocky valley of Tripsdale, uninhabited and well worth exploring. The finest bilberries I have ever found grow there. At this stage you might approve the suggestion that the name is derived from O. E. *thripel an instrument of torture, whilst Urra possible comes from O.E. horh*, filth – but Ura is the Celtic heather goddess.

Since the first edition there have been many changes on Urra Moor. The guiding line across was once given by tufts of moor grass

26

lying along the line of the old pack horse track. There were also some boundary stones, some only a century old, some very ancient indeed. In the winter of 1960-61 Lyke Wake walkers reported that a bull-dozer was tearing out a fire-break right across the moor and had damaged surviving portions of the paved causeway which was the next landmark further on. Representations were immediately made to the Estate and to the N.R.C.C. In the autumn of 1961 a working party of Club members restored damaged portions of the paved causeway and excavated considerable lengths of it not previously known to exist. The fire-break remains and is now a broad highway over the moor, visible ahead soon after Carr Ridge is climbed, and with one branch going down to Bilsdale Hall. Very little of the causeway is now visible.

Opposite the round barrow and survey pillar – 'Round Hill' – which mark the summit, is the Hand Stone, the rough carving of a hand on each side, pointing *This is the way to Stoxla and This is the way to Kirbie and . . .*' The stone, like others elsewhere, probably dates from 1711 when the Justices sitting at Northallerton ordered that guide posts should be erected throughout the North Riding. A short way on is another stone, the Face Stone. This is certainly much older. It has a sinister Celtic-style face deeply cut on the east side.

In a 1642 Perambulation of the Helmsley Estate boundaries occurs this:

> From Lambe Folde Stones goeinge N. to the Crosse with the Hande. (N.B. not the Hand Stone mentioned above). And soe forward to Bagerstone (the Badger Stone can be seen to the S. just below the source of Hodge Beck) leaueinge Cookinge (Cockayne) Rigg beeing the land of the Lord Duke of Buckingham on the East. And so goeinge N. wards vpp Barney Gill to the Streete Way. Then turninge N.W. to the bounder called Faceston.

Beyond a marshy piece where the fire-break curves round a little is another stone called the Red Stone or Rud Stone.

The present stone must have replaced a much older one. The name Red or Rud has several possible derivations. It is unlikely to mean red. It might be from Rood, a cross. It may be much older. **Redover** was an ancient name (Rievaulx Abbey Charters) for Hodge Beck which rises here – and this name probably comes from Welsh **rhed,** course, run, race; or **rhyd,** ford. Then the upright wooden stake in an old cow-house is called a rud-stake. And there is the Rudstone monolith in the E.R.

Near the Rud stone occur the first surviving flags of the paved Causeway, which from the above quotation clearly existed as an old paved causeway – Streete – in 1642. The Rud Stone is in fact a cross road with the ancient tracks from Helmsley by Baxtons and Rowpa and from Beadlam Rigg (the perambulation route) mentioned in the Rievaulx Cartulary 1145. The route from Beadlam was probably the Thurchilsti or Thorkil's Sty (**stee** is still good Cleveland dialect for a ladder or steep path) and this went on from the Rud Stone along what is now Turkey (Thorkil's) Nab.

The paved causeway is locally known as the sailors' or smugglers' trod. That it was used by smugglers is fairly certain, but it probably existed before smuggling became profitable. Packhorses were the main method of transport in medieval times. The track may have had older origins still – the Brigantes probably used pack horses – but though the crossing must be an ancient one, lying as it does along a line of drier moor, with very wet and boggy moor only a hundred yards to the north, and springs coming out lower to the south, the age of the paving stones beyond the 16th century can only be conjecture.

Much of the paving must have been taken by farmers. Some flags from the surviving sections were built years ago into shooting butts. Short lengths of track can be followed down to Bloworth Slack and beyond it on the south of the railway to Bloworth Crossing. The probability is that it then went down Farndale where on some maps there is a place marked Long Causeway.

NOTE: Do not make the mistake of letting your support party (unless in Churchill tanks) go up or down Turkey Nab or Monket Bank (the track from Rudland Rigg into Farndale).

At Bloworth Crossing is another ancient road, going down Rudland Rigg to Kirkbymoorside, with branches into Bransdale and Farndale. Beyond this, as the line curves left, there is a sudden dramatic change. At one end of a cutting you are looking down Bransdale; at the other you have crossed the narrow ridge and are looking down into Farndale. Every dale is lovelier than the last. Another magnificent round tour to do, particularly in daffodil time, is to come over Botton Head, as you have just done, and leave the railway anywhere now, but the easiest descent is down Middle Head, into Farndale, and down the river Dove to Low Mill – six miles of daffodils – then back by the track across Bransdale and Tripsdale to William Beck Farm just below Chop Gate, returning to Broughton by Cold Moor Rigg. 'Farndale' is possibly from Gaelic *Fearna*, alder.

The Rosedale Ironstone Railway is a fascinating bit of work. Iron Age man probably worked the Rosedale iron-ore, but in 1328 Edward III granted land for that purpose to the Rosedale Abbey nuns. Five hundred years later samples were turned down by Tyneside Ironmasters. They wrote that they were ashamed to see it lying on their quay! But with the Tees-side boom, Rosedale ore was found to be magnetic ore of excellent quality. Several thousand tons were carted to Pickering, then railed to Consett Ironworks, in Durham, for experiment. George Leeman, M.P., took the lease of Rosedale. He was Deputy Chairman of the N.E.R., and his associate

Sheriff was Traffic Manager. In 1861 the Rosedale branch was opened. Five million tons of ore were taken out in the first 20 years, but less than half that was removed in the next forty. An article in the *Manchester Guardian*, November 9th, 1928, *Twenty Miles of Railway to be taken up*, remarked sadly that for the last few months trains had run only twice a week. The seams had worn thin, and there was depression in Middlesbrough, so that the line was to be demolished by T.W. Ward Ltd., of Sheffield. Incidentally, at the height of the boom, a rival company had projected building a line from Leeds right up Bilsdale, with a tunnel through Ingleby Bank, under Hagg's Gate!

After numerous bends, there is a long straight stretch of track over a mile long, with Esklets at the head of Westerdale on the left. 'Gin Garth' on Westerdale Moor above Hob Hole is said to have been a storehouse for smugglers who crossed this way into Farndale, but the site was used for iron smelting and the 'gin' was probably an engine.

An old pile of lime at the side of the track indicates a route problem ahead. The O.S. maps still show what is a dry route over South Flat Howe joining "Jackson's Road" a little South of Old Margery, an apparently Celtic stone on the Castleton Rigg-Blakey Rigg road. This was our original route, but without our knowledge the Feversham Estate managed to get it excluded from the definitive paths. Later the Estate suggested we use the path from the lime pile down to Esklets, and the path/cart road from that farm to Old Margery. Though this cart road was also not a definitive path, it was a very ancient route, since Esklets was once a grange of Rievaulx Abbey. The old farm-house, inhabited till the 1940's, often provided shelter in the early years of the walk though it has since been demolished. Many walkers followed the old Cleveland Boundary stones from further along the railway direct to Old Margery. The early part of this route however is through a spring line, and there were some badly trodden boggy areas. The present owner of Westerdale Moor appears to object to walkers using any of these routes, and wants them to go right round by Blakey Inn, which (if support parties are at Rosedale Head / Old Margery) adds nearly three miles to the route. I personally recommend this, going on along the line for two miles beyond the Esklets track till just past Blakey Gill a short and easy path leads up to the Lion Inn, but only (a) if the inn is open and you need a drink, or (b) if you intend to avoid the detour back round the hard road by dropping down to the line again round the head of Rosedale, and then up the flagged

(George Gap) Causeway to rejoin the main Lyke Wake route at the Causeway Stone. (See Lyke Wake Way chapter). In my view, either the old path over South Flat Howe should be made definitive, or the path by the Boundary Stones should have walkways put through the boggy stretches. Meanwhile the Esklets alternative should surely remain.

If, one way or the other, you have arrive at Old Margery, you can avoid the road again (unless your support party are waiting at Ralph Cross) by taking a track across Wether Hill direct to Fat Betty, a rotund but charming white cross set in the heather a few yards north of the Rosedale road. This forms part of a line of white boundary stones which, if you wish to avoid the next two miles of road, you can happily follow. Indeed when they cross the road a second time just past the Fryup Head by-lane, and bend towards Loose Howe (1,419 ft.) they are your guide for three good miles across moor and bog to Shunner Howe.

Just past Loose Howe you will cross the George Gap causeway and a stone marked *Causeway Stone, 1864.* This is another of the tracks used by smugglers from the coast coming up through Great Fryup Dale and down into Rosedale. The marsh in the hollow below needs careful negotiating. From Loose Howe you may catch your first glimpse of the three radomes of Fylingdales E.W.S. beyond Shunner Howe.

Half your journey is now over and here some Lyke Wake wag raised a cairn and cross with the following inscription:

> *Poor old chap, he did try hard;*
> *He died to get his Dirger's card;*
> *Here he lies now, just half way;*
> *And here he'll stay for many a day.*

(The cairn, like him, has since sunk into the bog.)

North of Shunner Howe (another fine Norse name) are vast peat deposits controlled by the Danby Court Leet, where farms in Glaisdale have rights to turbary. We had the grazing at Glaisdale Head Farm in 1955 and it was while cutting peat here one loely August day, with the heather purple all around, that the idea of the Lyke Wake Walk occurred to me. Unfortunately all this area was burned in 1976 and is now the site of an experimental Moorland Management Scheme. By the time you have come down from Shunner Howe to Hamer you will actually have covered 23 miles with 17 still to go. If you make straight for the ruins you will have to wade through deep heather. Keep to the track by the boundary stones, which is, incidentally, the old Cleveland boundary all this way, and the going will be easy on to the road. Hamer is a good point for a support party to meet you, but camping is not permitted.

The old inn is a sad ruin now, its fields gone back to moor. The last occupant, George Boddy, died there in 1936, but there are still members of the family lower down at Hartoft who run their sheep up here. Indeed, one member of the family, now a schoolteacher, has done the walk. In the old days this was a very flourishing inn in summer, and often a saver of lives in winter, though there are stories of some who didn't reach it, but perished in the snow in Wintergill or by Bluewath Beck. One old man travelled around selling corks. His bleached bones, identified by the scattered corks, were found near an ancient sheepfold when sheep were washed in the hot days of summer. Joseph Ford, who was born at Hamer in 1870 and died at Castleton in 1944, tells this story in his Reminiscences, for his mother was a good customer of the old man. One night two young men, Atkinson and Eddon, died mysteriously in one of the rooms, over-powered it was supposed by fumes from newly-plastered walls. They are buried at Rosdale Abbey.

Until about 1870 there was often heavy traffic past Hamer, for this was one of the main roads from the south up to Egton and Whitby; hence the names of London Ho. and York Ho., farms in Glaisdale. In addition, the Hamer coalpits (marked now by mounds of shale behind the inn) were in full swing. Farmers from Glaisdale and Eskdale took wagon-loads of coal to Cropton and Hutton-le-Hole, bringing loads of lime back for their fields. It was poor quality coal, and in a thin seam – about 1ft. 8in. You can still find plenty lying around, and it burns all right! It was drawn to the surface in curfs (strong boxes) by a horse-wheel. As many as 20 wagon teams might be drawn up at Hamer then. A famous man who must have frequently called here was Captain Scoresby, the navigator, who lived at Cropton, and who drew many of his crew from there for whaling expeditions from Whitby – men who quarried lime in winter and hunted whales in summer; who carried great whalebones back with them to Cropton, and who once fought off the Press Gang in Whitby harbour, and probably celebrated their triumph here at Hamer.

And now ahead of you is the crux of the whole walk. Coming over Shunner Howe you would be able to see much of your route ahead – Simon Howe beyond the great sweep of Wheeldale Moor, and just to the left of Simon Howe, but far beyond, Lilla Howe, which marks the final stretch to Ravenscar. To the south of these lie

31

the tabular hills in an imposing phalanx, Broxa and Blakey, Levisham, and Leaf Howe with its thin rectangle of trees, now in deep forest.

It is the moor ahead, Wheeldale, which can break your heart and lame your legs. There is a good track now by Blue Man i' t' Moss, but avoid Wheeldale Gill (afforested). Or from Hamer go south-east to the intake wall corner, then, turning more easterly, you will see two rooks (piles) of stones more or less in line. Keep to this line until you see the High Pinkney shooting box, which must be kept a few hundred yards to your right. (It provides good shelter in case of need.) Take care that you have not gone too far south to the other shooting box on Middleton Moor. You should now strike a track which goes almost northerly for a short way then veers east along the long nose of Wheeldale Moor until it reaches the Stape Road. Go straight across this and down to the Roman road – 'Wade's Causeway', or the 'Old Wife's Trod' – a first century link between Cawthorn Camps and the coast near Whitby. A Y.H.A. sign indicates the track down to the delightful stepping stones across Wheeeldale Beck below the Lodge, a pleasant place for a short halt whether by sunlight or moonlight.

Coming down from Wheeldale Moor you will already have picked your line almost straight from the stepping stones up Howl Moor on to Simon Howe. The place names hereabouts are full of historic interest, particularly Wardle Rigg, to the south. In the Yorkshire Inquisition of 1252 it is 'Waldel' Rigg – the Rigg above the dale of the Welshmen, *wal* being from *wealh*, the Anglo-Saxon term for the Britons. This suggests, therefore, that a colony of Britons was still inhabiting this wild part in Anglo-Saxon times, and as late as when the parish boundaries were laid down, since the Blue Man is in all probability the British/Welsh *plu*, parish, and *maen*, stone, or parish boundary stone, as it still is. you will also find hereabouts Brown Howe and, further on the route, Brown Hill. There are other Brown Hills, elsewhere on the moors, often tipped with barrows; *Bron* is Welsh for a breast. Compare Brown Willy in Cornwall and the Pap of Glencoe.

Beyond Simon Howe down the left-hand side of Crag Stone Rigg there is easy downhill going on springy moss to Fen Bogs on the Newtondale railway. There is a very easy crossing here to Ellerbeck, but if you strike this line anywhere else you may have great difficulty crossing the bogs, particularly at Fen House. Both Fen Bogs and Fen House are deserted ruins now. (This area is now a nature reserve).

Lyke Wake Walk country – the panorama from Carr Ridge looking west to Hasty Bank. (Photo: Malcolm Budden)

Above: "Well, where do you think we are?" – Mal and Mike suffer from nocturnal doubts on one of the far-flung reaches of the Lyke Wake Walk.

Opposite, top: Green Howe, above Chop Gate, on the Southern Route, looking north to Cringle Moor and Cold Moor on the Classic Route.

Opposite, bottom: A stone near Green Howe, above Raisdale. This view also looks north to Hasty Bank as well as Cringle Moor and Cold Moor.

Above: Vanessa Clarke at Lilla Cross. She was the first Lyke Wake witch to do a triple crossing.

Opposite: Fat Betty, one of the most distinctive of the many stones and stone crosses on the North York Moors. (Photo: Malcolm Budden).

The author and "Rick" above Bilsdale.

Coming down from Botton Head with Carr Ridge, Hasty Bank, Cold Moor and Cringle Moor ahead.

Ski crossing of the Lyke Wake Walk in March 1986.

Members of the York Cross-Country Ski Club reach Lilla Cross. (Photos: Anne Blakemore).

Lyke Wake country at its bleakest as seen on Cringle Moor. (Photo: Malcolm Budden).

Round Newtondale Well a mid-summer Fair was held. The Scar was also celebrated for hawks. In 1612 a Crown Commission into the privileges and extent of the Lordship of the Royal Manor of Goathland reported that "There hath been hawkes bred in Newton Dale on Killingnoble Scar, which the inhabitants of Goathland were charged to watch for the King's use".

Fylingdales Moor was in military occupation for many years. In October 1958, some soldiers who were clearing the southern part of the moor were killed but no dangerous objects have been reported since 1970.

The direct route lies to the right of Little Ellerbeck stream, and walkers must be careful not to follow the main stream round to the south. Lilla Howe is the smaller of the two Howes you now see ahead, and is surmounted by Lilla Cross, reputed to be the oldest Christian monument on these moors, recalling an act of heroism in the 7th century.

The Cross had been moved to Sil Howe for safety during Army occupation and was returned to its proper home by Dirger Graham Leach, Whitby R.D.C. Engineer, in the summer of 1962. From Lilla Howe strike due east well to the right of Burn Howe Duck Pond. Make east for Burn Howe, and do not be tempted by the slope to Blea Hill and the sight of trees and fields beyond – a view which in misty conditions is so irresistible as to make the most experienced moorman think for a moment that his compass is wrong! Equally, do not be attracted by the slopes into the Derwent basin on the right. Cross the ravine of Jugger Howe beck at the corner where the beck turns east, and on the other side you can follow an army road to the Whitby-Scarborough road one mile south of the Flask Inn. From there the final long mile of track goes straight over Stony Marl Moor to the Beacon. The Beacon is now accepted as a finish in order to keep people out of Ravenscar village.

For a long time we thought that the Early Warning Station being built on Fylingdales would completely block the Classic route. Fortunately its boundary fence is south of Little Ellerbeck, though that section of land is retained by the Air Ministry. The Classic route may be adhered to, and on an easterly crossing the Warning Station buildings do not obtrude as much as we feared, though the spoliation of this wild and lovely moor is a matter for profound regret.

THE JOURNEY of the BRACKLEIANS
by T. D. Richards

A cold, frosty morning we had of it,
Just the right time of the year
For a journey, and such a long journey.
The bogs deep and the going hard
The very midst of Spring.
There were times we regretted
Leaving the warmth of our beds
And the toast and coffee and bacon and eggs.
Then the support party, cursing and grumbling
And rushing away, and wanting their beer and steaks,
And torches going out and the lack of shelter
and hostile hills and unfriendly boglands,
A bloody hard time we had of it.
At the end we crawled our way
Crying desperately for sleep
With voices crowing in our ears
That this was all folly

Then at dawn we came to Eller Beck,
Cold and wet, smelling of peat bog,
With running streams and Fylingdales humming in the darkness,
And three other ramblers on the low skyline,
And a support party racing on to final point.
Then we passed the golf balls caged by wire
With eager hands searching for dextrose tablets,
And sore feet plodding through peat bogs.
But there was no rest, and so we continued
And arrived at evening, not a moment too soon,
Finding the place; it was (you may say) satisfactory.

And all this was but a short time ago, I remember,
And I would do it again, but set down this,
Set down this. Were we led all that way
For Condolence Cards??? There was pain certainly,
We had blisters and aching thighs to prove it. I have been through
   pain
Before, but this was different. This pain was
Hard and bitter agony for us, like Death, on earth.
We returned home knackered
But no longer at ease here, in the old dispensation,
With an alien people clutching their easy life.
I should be glad of another Lyke Wake Walk.

Lyke Wake Walkers

BRONZE Age men must have been very familiar with the Lyke Wake route. William the Conqueror was lost for a night near Botton Head. Part of the Roman Ninth Legion disappeared without trace. In 1323 Edward II covered most of the route on a hunting trip, finishing with a feast at Whorlton Castle. His host, Nicholas de Meynell, must have done a double crossing when he carried off Lucia de Thweng from Mulgrave Castle.

Many of the 500 crossings reported between 1955 and 1960 are now the stuff of legend. In 1962 the Rev. A.E.C. Morgan completed a crossing just after his 81st. birthday, becoming the Club's Cheerless Chaplain at many Wakes till his death some ten years later.

One man's coffin badge was seen at Liverpool University and he was appointed Chief Technical Adviser in a water speed race in coffins against a London college. An argument as to which way coffins should be propelled for maximum efficiency aroused the interest of the Professor of Fluid Mechanics and models were tested in a pressurised wind tunnel. The answer was, appropriately, feet first. Another veteran dirger attended a TUC conference at Blackpool, to be greeted warmly by a hotel manager "ah, I recognise your badge, sir . . We have a lot of your members here-the Undertakers' Union isn't it?" At least two undertakers have done the walk – being persuaded that they might be needed in a professional capacity.

In the first two months of 1963 snow covered the moors, all roads were blocked, and people had to be rescued from the newly erected Early Warning Station. Conditions were perfect for the first ski-crossing.

We set off from Ravenscar Station at 1 p.m. on March 2nd – W. Cowley, J. Cowley, C. Bosanquet and D. Rich. Jugger Howe Ravine was the first exciting run – and stiff climb. Probably no one had been there, or on many other parts of the route, since the 'Longest Night crossing' which two of the present party had been on.

Fylingdales was a vast Arctic tract, sloping down to the snowy Derwent basin. A hazy sun glared on the snowfields with a Himalayan effect. We saw grouse and fox-tracks, and in addition to our own previous ski-tracks, two new ones which perturbed us. (We found later they were made by J. Wastling and A. Mathieson, Wilton I.C.I., who had started from Ravenscar just before dawn and reached Bloworth at sunset. They finally gave up at Carlton Bank after struggling a long time in the darkness). There was a long gentle run down from Lilla Cross (we could have stepped over the E.W.S. fence in several places) to Ellerbeck and on with a final swoop to Fen Bogs. Then as the sun set, on into Goathland for a night's rest at Church Farm.

On Sunday we climbed up to Two Howes again as the sun rose behind the three giant puff-balls of the E.W.S. It was a remarkable and I will admit quite beautiful sight in those conditions. A long slanting run down to the Stepping Stones, and Wheeldale Moor was excellent going in the crispness of the morning. Even the deepest heather was a level snowfield. So was the bog beyond Hamer. From Loose Howe another long delightful run took us swooping down to the old line in Rosedale, which was like a Himalayan valley. Blakey at noon – and the road had been opened nearly to the inn that morning. The Bosanquet family had fought their way up with delicious stew to accompany the 'Lion's' beer.

From there we skied in an ecstasy of snow and sun over South Flat Howe and down to the railway. We cut out some of its curves, preferring to climb a little for the sake of the run down. At Bloworth two or three walkers struggling through deep snow eyed us enviously. We took the fire-break to Chop Gate knowing the five steep climbs on the classic route would now be beyond our strength (though they had provided magnificent ski-ing on another day). The descent to Bilsdale Hall, where south-facing snow had melted then frozen, was exciting in the extreme. Apart from two or three short steep climbs the few hundred yards of main road from Seave Green was the only time we carried our skis. Unorthodox routes over drifted walls and hedges took us up on to Scugdale Moor. We went across the middle of Brian's Pond. Frozen solid and snow covered it was difficult to distinguish form the Arctic tundra all around. The sun was setting and the wind was bitter. Down through Snotterdale, a last tedious climb, and a hazardous run in the dark back to Swainby, and right to our door-step at Potto Hill – 7 p.m. 17 hours ski-ing, 30 hours altogether. On Monday the thaw set in – we had been only just in time.

No other ski-crossing was reported till 1981, Dec. 28th and 29th, by Price and Patterson, 19 hours, with a bivouac in Arctic conditions in Northdale Gully. With the increasing popularity of Nordic cross-country ski-ing, there have been several since. With the route so well-trodden now, it would not need a very heavy snow-cover to make the route feasible. Three members of the Cleveland Mountaineering Club crossed successfully on February 22nd in 15¾ hours. (R. O'Callaghan) Anne Blakemore was the first woman to do a ski-crossing, with three members of the York Ski-Club, March 1 and 2 that same year, in 18 hrs. 10. mins ski-ing time, with a stop at Blakey. Andrew Leader, Karen and Mitch Wilson did an ordinary crossing in 13 hours on Dec. 29 1986 and a ski-crossing on Jan. 16 and 17 1987 in 19 hours.

Three crossings have been completed in the hours of darkness, between sunset and sunrise in December. At least two have been done in wheelchairs, with assistance, and one extraordinary crossing by an indomitable spastic, John Hawkridge, in four days at his fourth attempt. Back at the Queen Catherine some customer thought that his slow progress on two sticks was the result of doing the walk "Oh, no" said the barmaid "he didn't walk any better than that when he started".

Flight Lt. Tait and two other R.A.F. officers after a double crossing in 38 hours wrote:

Pain! A simple exercise in enduring pain. Aching, cut and blistered feet. Creaking knees that crack and cry stop. Bits of moving skin which rub painfully against other bits that don't. Even those parts of the body that dont't do anything go stiff and sore through prolonged inactivity. The terrible suffering of going downhill, the almost overpowering effort of going uphill, is only matched by the need to persuade the body to go on at all. It is worth all the suffering. The pleasure of achievement; the knowledge that you can do something which few others have the endurance to do. More important, the simplicity of it all, just walking, mixed with a little food and sleep. Escape from modern complex society to simple problems. A beautiful sunrise, desolate moorland, and tinned pineapple juice. Young grouse, flowering heather, and sitting on the edge of a stream with the water rushing between your toes. It is worth the pain. Your companions are tedious. They walk too fast or too slow. They say the wrong things or don't talk when they ought to. Suffer from different aches and problems and don't seem bothered about yours. Yet when the going is really bad one of them will always fill a gap, be cheerful when it's needed, or find the right track when you are lost. The support party. An excuse for a rest, a legitimate reason to stop, just for a moment. But they don't understand. They don't understand why you are early, or late, or why you are limping or moaning, or, really, how you get from one check point to the next. But they are vital, your contact with outside, someone you can scream at without offending.

Group Capt. Wright, C.O. Fylingdales R.A.F., and Mrs Wright did the walk in June. It was a clear sunny morning and they felt a sense of foreboding when they realised they had to walk three times as far as the eye could see. Barbara Wright nearly gave up at Wheeldale 'but the thought of having to go through the whole agony again drove us on'.

An R.A.F. party in June 1974 included Air Vice-Marshall C.G. Maughan, C.B.E., A.F.C., who completed the walk in 10 hours 55 minutes. Another joint R.A.F./R.N. party in October was led by Group Capt. D. Palmer, O.B.E. On Wheeldale one of the party thought he could see the sea but on closer inspection was dismayed to find it was Wheeldale Beck running full and wide. They found that the agony of descending to Jugger Howe ravine was only surpassed by the hell of climbing out of it.

Sq. Leader Hurrell A.F.C. reached the Raven Hall Hotel, but

someone had to take his money to the bar for him, as having sat down he couldn't get up: 'I admire your judgment in selecting just the right length for the walk. Many in the bar shared my view that if the bar had been five yards further east you'd be short of a lot of completions.'

The walk has always inspired those who complete it to peaks of literary achievement, like the party who "approached Simon howe like Old Testament prophets arriving at Mount Tabor" The Duke of Devonshire claims – safely – to be the oldest Duke to have done the walk. He did it when he was 60 and is rightly proud of his Lyke Wake tie. There have been Chief Constables and Juvenile delinquents, bell-ringers and bookmakers, blind men and boxers. Amongst others especially noted were fourteen bottle sorters from the National Glassworks, three Artificial Inseminators from the Cattle Breeding Centre at York, a coxless eight of the Bedford Rowing Club; Hawkins Slimming Systems International, Bortofts Crumpets, Manufacturers of Hot Plate Goods, Scarborough; a Metropolitan Fraud Squad (who issued a warrant for the Chief Dirger's arrest under Section 18, Offences against the Person Act, 1861, to be brought before the Bar of The Lamb in Holborn, unless he appeared voluntarily, which he did, claiming Manorial Privilege, Droit de Seigneur, and Benefit of Clergy (as pleaded by Nicholas de Meynell in a similar case in 1330); a group of York Centenary Circuit Methodists and the English Martyrs Church, York; various fire brigades, Customs and Excise, Blood Transfusion Service, Melton Mowbray postmen, Kossett Carpets, Charterhouse School, Colne Operatic Society and a group from the Royal Canadian Horse Artillery. The novelist Mark Adlard, having re-read Pilgrim's Progress, thought that John Bunyan also must have crossed Loose Howe at some time: 'Now a great mist and darkness fell upon them. Here was but sorry going, the way very wearisome. Nor was there so much as one inn or victualling house, wherein to refresh the feebler sort.'

The Police Central Planning Unit, Harrogate, made detailed preparations as to logistics and communications, but finished the walk like Napoleon's retreat from Moscow. Dr. Manning, of Whitney, did the walk because he thought the tie would be very suitable for a general practitioner. The Northern Ombudsman and staff from York were followed by Lord John Oaksey and other members of the 'Press gang'. The Wards sent up a prayer from the

Rosedale bog –

> 'Water, water everywhere
>   and we are wading through it;
> O Thou who walked on water,
>   give us the strength to do it.'

On New Year's leave from Nigeria, Roger Withers going west-east lost a camera. Professor Swanson of Surrey going east-west met him, failed to find the camera, but noticed fresh footprints going east. Brian Mills of Guiseley (going east) found the camera in four inches of frozen water and eventually it reached its owner. Withers, back in Nigeria (having given up exhausted when a farmer near Blakey offered him a lift), went on a camel trek, decided camels might be the answer to the Lyke Wake Walk, and started a new line in T-shirts – 'Lyke Wake Walk Failed'. He crossed, without camel, on his next leave. Peter Parkinson took his wife Laurie on one section of the walk in pouring rain hoping to cure her of any desire to do it, but no – she was 'absolutely fascinated by the beauty, the wildness and the splendour' and insisted on accompanying him on a full crossing.

Michael Dean, consultant surgeon, watched the European Games after his crossing and felt amazed that you could get a medal for a mere 100 yards dash, whilst even the marathon was only 26 miles!

Five disabled members of Finchale College took 20 hours to reach Ravenscar and one hour cutting themselves out of their seized-up artificial limbs.

Charlie Thomson of Leeds led a party of six and the youngest of them was 50. Charlie is 53, 6ft. 3ins, 18 stone, and promised a donation to the Club funds if any member was taller, older, and heavier than him! At 5 a.m. on a cold May morning J.R. Carter's party passed a man asleep in a deck chair on Blakey Ridge. Another party in July passed several bodies at the same place laid out in polythene bags. A French girl Mlle. Savoye, wrote that she 'enjoyed the walk in spite of the blisters, because it gave confidence and found out what my possibilities were'.

Eleven representatives of Ladbrokes the bookmakers walked for Cancer Research: 'All were overweight and unhealthy. Of the field, four set off at a tremendous gallop and soon had a good lead, with the rest of the bunch settling in behind. The first obstacle, Live Moor, took its toll and at Hasty Bank Jimmy, the locally trained stallion, who had obviously been overworked, collapsed, as did Keith, who had too much weight to carry and was handicapped to lose anyway. Several more dropped out at the Rosedale Bend. At Shunner Howe, Dave from Redcar lost his shoes in the mire and without a blacksmith had to be retired. There were just two finishers.'

P. Belshaw reported 'yet another lapse into masochism – the third in 18 days. My toes have now turned a funereal purple under the nails, like ripe damsons in the fall, and soon I fear they will drop off'.

On his fourth crossing in May with his wife, he came across an extraordinarily moving scene. Round the starting pillar were the bodies of some half dozen successful moonlight Dirgers, slumped in complete abandon, like baggage awaiting collection. "Out of respect we spoke in whispers and tiptoed away. We left this Henry Moore group with the sun shining in a flawless sky, and a spectacular mist inundating the valley below like a petrified Arctic Sea."

Paul Mallet found this book highly entertaining before he did the walk but whenever he looks at it now sick feelings sweep over him. Alan Hoffman heard about the walk in Sydney – and became the first Australian to do it! Northallerton was the first Young Farmers' Club to complete the walk. D.W. West of Marton composed a prayer:

> Thank Him above for feet so trim,
> And size 9 boots to put them in;
> For tracks and trods that reach so far
> Across the hills to Ravenscar.
> Oh keep those hills as they were then,
> A place for silent walking men!

Another poet provided this appropriate parody:

> 'Twas brillig, and the dirgers three
> Did mesh and werble in the vast;
> All mimsy was the croaky knee
> And the moan gasps outpassed.
>
> Beware the Lyke Wake Walk, my son!
> The miles that grind, the heather hell!
> Beware the glugsuck bog, and shun
> The frumjious unexploded shell!.

Amongst many schools that do the walk regularly are King's, Rochester and Westminster, Mill Hill, Cundall Manor, and

Earlham School, Norwich, from which 200 boys have crossed in 9 years. Brian Robinson spent his 11th. birthday on the walk and has been back every year since; introducing many others to the moors "Which has given me so much pleasure .... and at times a fright".

Following the examples of the Mayors of Beverley and Barnsley, and the Sheriff of York amongst other Municipal Representatives, the Mayor of South Tyneside and some of his Councillors and staff crossed in September 1987 and presented their artist's impression of the walk to the Club's Black Art Gallery.

What seems a very appropriate crossing was done in September 1988 by David Ing, Master of the Worshipful Company of Woolmen, sponsored by members of his Livery.

Two poems by G.T. Robinson (from a Thesis for the degree of Doctor of Dolefulness).

1.
How green is Greene Howe?
Not very green.
All brown and dirty.
No green's to be seen
Green Howe's not green.

How flat is Flat Howe?
Not very flat.
Climb up from Esklets–
You're satisfied that
Flat Howe's not flat.

How Loose is Loose Howe?
Too bloody loose.
Proof is the bog juice.
And crucified boots.
Loose Howe is loose.

2. A PLEA TO THE SEA
O mighty pounding sea,
Please do a favour for me.
Erode those cliffs away
At distant Robin Hood's Bay.
Produce a new coast far
Away from Ravenscar.
O sea I'd love to see
You here at Osmotherley.

G.T. Robinson did his 26th crossing in April 1978' More of his verses appear in Lyke Wake Lamentations. He is the author of *Feats for Feet*, two hard walks in Teesdale. (Teesdale Mercury Ltd., Barnard Castle).

Lyke Wake Club

The Lyke Wake Club must be unique in that it has no formal organisation and no subscription. It has been likened to a tribal society, the only entry into which is by ordeal! All who do the walk in the conditions laid down become members (or "Dirgers") and there are no honorary ones. The Club confines its activities to collecting information about the walk. It is also concerned, however, with encouraging members to learn all they can about the moors, their history and folk-lore, and to assist in safeguarding them. Circulars are issued as necessary to members who send a stock of stamped and addressed envelopes, and no reply can be sent to any communication unless a stamped and addressed envelope is enclosed. Before attempting the walk please send for the latest circulars. All who do the walk and wish to claim membership of the Club must send an account of their walk, with details of route and time, plus 20p per head (and s.a.e.) to the Chief Dirger, Swainby, Northallerton. A black-edged Card of Condolence is sent in acknowledgement of successful crossings, and badges may be bought.

Reports may be pungent or poetic – we welcome quotable ones – but if purely factual should be as brief as possible. The charge of (at present) 20p for Condolence Cards represents the cost, not of the card only, but of the clerical expense of handling reports and keeping statistics. Please report all crossings. A special card is now available for double crossings (both ways within 48 hours) 30p. You can save money by doing a double crossing!

The Club has gradually built up, with more humour than seriousness, its own rather macabre traditions based on the Lyke Wake Dirge and other Cleveland folk-lore. The crest is a silver coffin and three silver tumuli (Ordnance Survey sign) on a black shield. The cloth badge is a silver candle and two tumuli on a black coffin. The tie is black, with silver coffins, candles and tumuli.

Women members, who may wear a black scarf with the above

badge, form the Circle of Witches. Their duty is to cast suitable spells and ward off the machinations of Hobs, Boggets, Gabriel Ratchets and the like. The Emblem of the club is the rowan – mountain ash, or witchen tree. This is to ward off the unsuitable spells of the witches. In explanation of some of this folk-lore see the story of the Glaisdale and Farndale Hobs, Atkinson's *Forty Years in a Moorland Parish*. There too, you will find much about the witches of this district who so frequently turned themselves into hares.

The Club mace, presented by Selby Round Table, is of polished rowan, with a facsimile of the Scarth Wood Survey Pillar at one end, and a coffin at the other.

From the early days of the Club a few enthusiasts used to gather at the *Queen Catherine* for what might be called a postmortem on the year's efforts. This became the Annual Winter Wake, now the Candlemas Wake. As only 60 seats are available, this Wake rapidly becomes crowded out; early application is essential though the menu might frighten many away. One reporter said he would walk 40 miles to avoid it! Witches' Broth, Hare Stew with Rowan Jelly, Crab Apple Pie, and Funeral Biscuits are the tradition.

The first Midsummer Wake was held at the *Lion Inn*, Blakey, on 24th June, 1961. subsequent ones till 1984 were at Potto Hill, where the Lyke Wake Olympics became a feature – Bog Jumping, Throwing the Stone Age Hammer and the Bronze Age Spear, the Witches Broomstick Race, and the Witches' Spell Casting Competition. For many years a Halloween Wake was also held at Potto Hill, when everyone had to come in historic, ghostly or ghastly dress. One year a group of Vikings with helmets, shields and battle-axes arrived, having apparently beached their longboat on the Durham coast, and sang the Lambton Worm at any pause in the proceedings. Sadly, Potto Hill is no longer available but Lyke Wake walkers may like to organise their own local Wakes elsewhere.

The correct dress for Wakes is of course black, but in default of this some suitable sign of mourning should be worn, and it should never be forgotten that the Wake is a solemn occasion. Any display of mirth is most unseemly, and sympathy should be indicated by deep and heart-felt groans. There should be no smoking until the loyal toast to Edward II after which churchwarden pipes may be produced. The Dirge is sung, the Centuries of the last Wake are read, and a Post-Mortem report on recent crossings presented.

Examinations may be conducted for the degree of Master of Misery, and theses delivered for that of Doctor of Dolefulness.

The 21st Anniversary Wake was appropriately held in the Haunted Castle, Kirby Misperton on 2nd October 1976. A Silver Jubilee Wake was held in the Potto Hall Hotel on October 4 1980, closely followed by an Extraordinary Wake on 14th November at Stones' Brewery in Sheffield. Anniversary Wakes have been held in 1981 at the Blacksmith's Arms, Hartoft and in 1982 on the Lincoln Castle Ferry, moored under the Humber Bridge, whilst 'Brewster Sessions' have been repeated in Sheffield. Wakes licensed (and occasionally graced) by Club officials have been held in Ossett, Oxford, London and other outposts of empire.

In 1988 the Toyne/Whittaker families organised a very successful Midsummer Wake at Hundred Acre Farm, Strensall, York, which is likely to be repeated, and the Club appears to have opened a London branch or Chapel of Ease at 32 Ravensdale Avenue, North Finchley (N12 9HT) from which Brian Piercy has organised London Wakes for the last four years.

People sometimes ask why we do not keep a closer time check of people doing the walk. For one thing, of course, it is impossible. But it is quite unnecessary. No one who attempts a walk of this kind is going to cheat. If he did, he would not last for half an hour at a Wake amongst people who know every inch of the way on every alternative route, and where details of routes and of weather are the main topic of conversation! Many people have reported failing by half a mile, some by a quarter of an hour. The challenge, and the satisfaction, are your own. It is this shared experience, of the same walk, perhaps not by quite the same route, and rarely in the same conditions, that gives a special basis of fellowship to the Lyke Wake Club. Incidentally, we are prepared to allow an extra 12 hours for every 5 years of age over 65!

There is perhaps no other walk which covers such a complete and well-defined stretch of hill country within the compass of one long day. So many people have done it a great many times that the Club has instituted an amusing – but none the less arduous – series of degrees. To become a Master (or Mistress) of Misery (black neckbands) you must do three crossings, one of which must be in the opposite direction, and attend two Wakes. To become a Doctor of Dolefulness (purple bands) you must do four more crossings, one of which must be between 1st December and 28th February and one unsupported. You must have attended four Wakes and must present a thesis on some aspects of the walk. One more degree is that of Past Master. He must have done some 15 crossings and have contributed great services to the Club. A Past Master should be able to find his way across any moor by day or night, drunk or sober, without map or compass. The first ten P.Ms. were: the Chief Dirger, A. Puckrin, C. Bosanquet, P.A. Sherwood, J.M. Cowley, J. Adams, E. Emberton, A. Waller, Wendy Long, and Mary Hunt.

The present hierarchy of the Club is constituted as follows:
The Most Mournful the Chief Dirger (and the Chief Witch)
The Melancholy Mace-bearer and the Horrible Horn-blower
The Misguided Foundation Members.
The Cheerless Chaplain.
The Anxious Almoner. (P. Morgan)
The Miserable Bier Carriers.
The Embittered Brewer (M. Parker of Stones)
The Wretched and Erroneous Recorder who keeps
the "Centuries" of each Wake.
The Harassed Archivists
The Pro-Vice-Chancellor, Eric Toyne, Chairman of the Court of Past Masters.
The Senile Centenarians
The Harmonious Minstrels (P. and M. Pedder).
Past Masters in order of Passing.
Doctors of Dolefulness in order of Dole.
Masters of Misery in order of Mastery.
Witches in order of Witchery.
Dirgers in order of Tribulation.

Esklets

There's a pleasant little ruin
   in the head of Westerdale,
Just below the white lime pile
   along the ironstone rail.
A tiny dancing beck nearby
   goes chattering bright and gay,
Running to the sea at Whitby
   downhill all the way.

But this easy downhill pathway, mate,
   is not for you and me,
Some twit thought up harder ways
   of getting to the sea.
You flog and slog up soggy, boggy
   moorland till you drop,
Leaving you a sweaty, smelly
   ruin at the top.

(G.T. Robinson)

Races and Records

IN 1957 Arthur Puckrin did a west-east crossing in 10 hr 10 min and the double in 23 hr 19 min. In 1961 Eric Derwin did 8.38 but almost immediately Arthur Puckrin replied with 6.40 for the full Classic route (R. Puckrin 7.16). The following year Arthur lowered this again to 6.19 and 16.17 for the double. Later he managed 6.13 (west-east Classic) and also did a triple (W/E, E/W, W/E) in 32.15 for the 120 miles. This included a time of 14.58 for the first two crossings, a record for the double till 1985).

Arthur has progressed through various editions of this book from Queen's Scout to Police Cadet, police constable, law student, barrister and business man whose main hobby is now bridge!

In 1968 J. Gray and L. Kulscar did four consecutive crossings in 78 hours.

Consternation and controversy were aroused when a runner claimed a time of 4.30 for the W/E crossing. He had one witness and a very strong following wind. Athletic circles refused to believe that some mistake had not been made in timing. A Harriers' Race was organised, W/E, and Mick McDonald set a new official record time of 6.1. In September 1970 international athletes M. Turner and C. Garforth of Cambridge University set up a new official W/E record for the full Classic route (Triangulation pillar on Scarth Wood Moor to Raven Hall Hotel Bar) of 4 hrs 58 mins 7 secs. This still stands.

In July 1964 however the Osmotherley Summer Games Committee (Osmotherley Village Games go back for many centuries) asked the Club to organise a Lyke Wake Race E/W in connection with the Games, to end at the village cross, and any profits to go to a fund for the new village hall. This race is therefore slightly different from the Classic route in that it starts at Beacon Howe Pylon above Ravenscar and finishes in Osmotherley. This is one-sixth of a mile longer than the Classic route but is otherwise fairly comparable in difficulty on the ground. A head wind is more likely to blow from the west and a strong wind could certainly make half an hour or more difference. Except perhaps in wet conditions the going is easier now than in early years. There is no heather to contend with, but more bog.

The race includes a handicap event as well as the fastest time. Arthur Puckrin had the fastest time in 1964 – 6.30. This was equalled by Jeff Hall in 1966. Wendy Long was the fastest woman with 11.07. In 1968 Philip Puckrin set up a new Race record of 5.15 and in 1971 5 hours. In 1978 the first five (out of 55 finishers) were under 6 hours. Brenda Yule lowered the women's record to 7.30. Audrey Collinson made this 7.17 the following year and Linda Lord has lowered it each year since – 7.04, 6.38, and 6.10 in 1982. In 1983 Brenda Yule made this 5.59 but Linda came back with 5.56 in 1985. For the first ten years of the race Arthur Puckrin or Philip Puckrin won every race but one. Only in 1979 did the great fell runner Josh Naylor get the record down to 4.53 with Mick Garratt of Guisborough just two minutes behind him. Mick won the following year in 5.09 but lowered the record in 1981 to 4.51. In 1986 Bob Mitchell made this 4.47. The Lyke Wake Shield is presented for the fastest crossing, the Ralph Stafford Memorial Cup to the fastest woman, and the Masterman Rose Bowl to the first on Handicap. Handicap winners have included J. Waind, A. Collinson, I.A. Cooper, R. Britton, B. Hingston, L. Kulscar, D. Oglesby, P.A. Sherwood and O. Pedder (1982, in 7.48, at age 14).

The Lyke Wake Shield was presented by Dick Thompson of Osmotherley for the first race in 1964 and carved by Thomas Brown of Middlesbrough. The Masterman Rose Bowl was presented the following year by Mrs Masterman in memory of her husband who competed in the first race. The Ralph Stafford Memorial Cup was presented by I.A. Cooper and P.A. Sherwood in 1980 in memory of a friend who was an active member of the Osmotherley Summer Games Committee for many years.

L. Kulscar was the first man to complete 100 crossings, on November 17, 1973. During 1974 he did six double crossings, one of them in 16 hrs 15 mins. Lewis escaped from Hungary in the crisis of 1956, cycling to the Austrian border. By chance he came to Teesside as a baker – and at the end of a night shift would escape again to the moors for fresh air and exercise! At least three of his crossings were done barefoot. His fastest was 6.40 – 'because it was too cold to stop'. He has now done 170 crossings. In the 1982 Race, three sons ran with him and two of them beat their father who only managed 10.15. His great friend, and a very popular member of the

Club, was John Gray, who completed 50 crossings before his tragically early death in 1974. One of John Gray's poems is on the first page of *Lyke Wake Lamentations*.

Second man to complete 100 crossings was Ben Hingston in October 1974. Ben's first crossing had been alone and unsupported in July 1966 when he spent some hours of the night on a mortuary table in Scarborough Police station, the only hospitality available. Thereafter he averaged a crossing every month, quietly becoming one of the outstanding and best-loved characters in the Lyke Wake Club. He did his 200th crossing on January 15, 1983, and his 212th . . . sadly, his last . . . on 9th February 1984. Cancer was already affecting his lungs and he died in October 1985, 65 years old. Later we scattered his ashes on Cringle Moor in deep snow and a howling gale, and held a special Wake in his honour. Typically he had arranged the programme himself and left money for the drinks! He used to hide cans of beer on the moor for use in the Race or some subsequent crossing, so some lucky dirger may still find a can of Ben's beer.

The third "Senile Centenarian" is Ian Ashley Cooper, who retired after his 157th crossing but still assists in the Race and at Wakes (fastest time 9.5). Coming up fast is the youngest of the Senile Centenarians, Gerald Orchard, 115 crossings at last count but liable to have done another double or triple since, and did the present record double of 14.4 on 20th July 1985 when his time for the first leg, E-W, was 5.8. He won the annual race in 1983 with 5.21 but is well behind the Race record of 4.47.

The leading lady in number of crossings is Margaret Toyne, whose husband, Eric, (wartime SAS) has retired at 37 crossings, the same as the Chief Dirger. Margaret did her 60th crossing on 22.6.88 at age 71. Their grandson Charles Whitaker has already done 34 crossings before his 18th birthday. He won the Masterman (handicap) Rosebowl in the 1985 race, and the George Ward Rosebowl the following year when his mother, the Toyne's daughter Susan, won the Masterman. Three other Toyne grandchildren are following this example.

Professor Alan Swanson used the night of the October full moon to celebrate his 50th birthday with a seventh, and what must be the most expensive crossing recorded – by train, bus and taxi from London at a cost of £46.89 for travel alone. A challenge on a 'high cost' basis might however come from Mr and Mrs Sainsbury who travelled from Canada in order to do the walk, and Mr Le Mesurier who has twice come from there to do crossings.

In September 1980 Mary and Trevor Wade were (probably) the first married couple to do a double crossing (33.50). V. Helm was the fourth man to do a triple (52.40, well outside A. Puckrin's 1962 record). In 1982 a family group of three generations of Bells and Dolans down to 8-year old M. Dolan crossed in 14 hours.

The youngest to cross has been Christopher Turton, at 6 years, 11 months, succeeding Heather Cowley (9) and Neil Brown (7½). Andrew Chapman did a second crossing at the age of 8. Julie Vine (13) became the youngest girl to do a double crossing, a feat equalled by Vanessa Clarke in 1987. A year later, at 14, Vanessa became the first girl of any age to do a triple crossing. (July 1988, from dawn on Thursday to 7.0 p.m. on Saturday). So far Vanessa has done eight crossings, the first with her mother, Dr. Margaret Clarke, and the last with her sister Valerie (12). We expect more from the family in future. In June 1988 ten boys and five staff from William Henry Smith School, Brighouse, did a double crossing. All the boys were under 16 and one only 13½. One other boy did the single crossing.

Boulders, bogs, becks and bombs
by G. T. Robinson (about 1960)

On Wainstones when the foot slips,
Crunch!
That battered shin will make you late for lunch.

On Rosedale when the foot slips,
Spludge!
That sunken boot is very hard to budge.

At Wheeldale Lodge when foot slips,
Splosh!
You're soaked, but still by now you need a wash.

On Fylingdales when foot slips,
BOOM!
You're doing ghostly dirges on the Moon.

(From "Lyke Wake Lamentations")

The Lyke Wake Way

MANY people have inquired whether it is possible to do the Lyke Wake Walk in a more leisurely way – in two or three days. The answer is yes, but it will not qualify for membership of the Lyke Wake Club. Additionally there is the difficulty of accommodation, which is seldom nearer than two miles away from the Classic route. In this chapter therefore I am suggesting a number of alternative routes, all on definitive footpaths, any combination of which would fall within the original definition of the Lyke Wake Walk except for 'Keeping to the tops as far as possible'. By going in to Chop Gate in Bilsdale, into Rosedale and Glaisdale, accommodation becomes available, and people who do not find a 40 mile challenge walk to their taste would find this a very enjoyable three day walk. I must stress again that these alternatives are not generally suitable for large parties, or for sponsored walks. They need careful map-reading, and pass through villages and small farms where too much disturbance would be very unwelcome. At the same time it will not escape anyone's notice that to follow the Classic Lyke Wake route to Rosedale Head, and then take the Trough House, Glaisdale, Wintergill, Struntry Carr, Beck Hole, York Cross alternative, makes it possible to do the Lyke Wake Walk acceptably on definitive or acknowledged footpaths which can never be closed except by general agreement in times of great fire risk (or shooting days perhaps). This would make the walk nearer to 50 miles than to 40, but it would be possible. Many parties claim to have done over 50 on the Classic route anyway! But it would be much easier to get lost on the alternatives, and then you might find yourself doing 60 miles or more. The 'Lyke Wake Way' is a very pleasant and varied route for small parties taking their time. We would like to have comments on the route and accommodation from anyone who does it.

BETWEEN OSMOTHERLEY AND ROSEDALE

I have already indicated some alternatives between Scarth Wood Moor and Chop Gate. It is very regrettable that there is no direct definitive footpath between Osmotherley and Chop Gate without going down into Snilesworth as far as Low Cote Farm. This can be done from Osmotherley by following the Cleveland Way up Oakdale, then some 2½ miles of road past Snilesworth Lodge gate. From Low Cote a footpath goes north-east below Rye Farm and up Arnsgill Ridge. Above Head House (empty) take the right hand fork for Cock Howe and down Trennet Ridge to Chop Gate. If however you have arranged to spend the night in Bilsdale at Fangdale Beck keep south from Cock Howe past Miley Howe to the Bilsdale Mast and drop down to Fangdale Beck from there. In either case the distance from start is just under ten miles.

Other alternatives are to turn off the Classic route either at Carlton Bank, south of the Glider station, and south down the long ridge past Brian's Pond to Cock Howe; or from Cold Moor south down 'Cawdma Rigg' into Chop Gate. (There seems to be no accommodation at present here, but there is the Buck Inn for meals).

From Chop Gate you would go through Seave Green to Bilsdale Hall from where a good track goes (south of the farm) E.N.E. over Urra Moor to rejoin the Classic route on Botton Head. From Fangdale Beck your best plan is to take the track by High or Low Crossett and across Bilsdale East Moor either by Bonfield Gill or by Basin Howe and 'Botany Bay' into Bransdale. You follow the minor road round the head of Bransdale, up onto Rudland Rigg and down into Farndale by Dickon Howe and Monket Bank. There is an inn – Feversham Arms – at Church Houses. From here you can go up the road to Blakey, and rejoin the high level routes, or better still, especially in daffodil time, take the field path down Farndale to Low Mill then either from Crag Cottage by Pike Howe into Thorgill or from Duck House by the 'Beggars' Track' over Three Howes into Rosedale Abbey direct.

There is plenty of accommodation in Rosedale. The distance from Bilsdale will vary from 12 to 16 miles according to the route.

FROM ROSEDALE TO RAVENSCAR

Anyone on the Classic route has a choice whether to turn off the old railway line just past the pile of lime and go through Esklets or over Flat Howe (boundary stones) to Old Margery and Rosedale Head; or to keep on the railway line till the track goes off to the Lion Inn at Blakey (a highly desirable call). Anyone in Farndale can also come up to Blakey.

From Old Margery a bridle path goes through the heather direct to Fat Betty (White Cross) at Rosedale Head, avoiding the road. A mile on the road south-east from Fat Betty is the Fryup Road turning (there is a path cutting the corner). Half a mile north along the Fryup road a good track turns off east for Trough House and on across Glaisdale Moor, round the head of Great Fryup Dale to Glaisdale Rigg.

Alternatively from Blakey you may drop down to the old railway line on the Rosedale side and go round the head of Rosedale on the line (this is not a definitive footpath but has been used by many people for many years) to a point above the second and lower Dale Head Farm where the George Gap Causeway, a bridle path, comes up from Rosedale. (Anyone in Rosedale would also make for here). From Blakey you can also take the definitive footpath south-east to still another (middle) Dale Head Farm, south to Hollin Bush, then east down a couple of fields and across a footbridge to the Dale Head Farm and the Causeway. This ancient Pannierman's (and Smugglers') Causeway heads north-east to Fryupdale and Lealholme, and thence to Staithes, Runswick or Sandsend, old smuggling ports all. It crosses the Classic route at 'Causeway Stone 1864' just west of the West Gill Bog. (Any Lyke Wake walker on the Classic route therefore, who wishes to avoid Rosedale head and Loose Howe, may take this route from Blakey, and rejoin the Classic route here. Still better, if he wishes to avoid a bog also, he can take a bulldozed track which leaves the Rosedale road a few yards south of the George Gap Causeway. This crosses south of the bog, where the bog has become a stream. Where the bulldozed track, now much eroded in places, turns south, a hundred yards of dry moor to the north lead back onto the Classic route on Middle Head, safely past the worst bogs.)

Those following the Causeway, however, keep on for a good half mile north-east across William Hill till the track from Trough House comes in from the left and the Causeway slants down into Fryup. At this point turn right along the Trough House track towards Cock Howe on Glaisdale Rigg, three-quarters of a mile away. The definitive path keeps north to join the Glaisdale Rigg nearly a mile further on, but a (careful) short cut by the shooting house will bring you out where you want to be, where the 'Common Lonnin' turns down to Yew Grange in Glaisdale Head. Mrs Lister at Yew Grange has accommodation (Whitby 87352) as has Mrs Clarke close by at Hutton Lodge (87433) but not in July/ August. There is more accommodation in Glaisdale village but the best way to get there would be to keep along Glaisdale Rigg taking the right-hand fork.

From Yew Grange the track goes by Readman House to Mountain Ash Farm and then curves up the steep ridge to the ruined farmhouse of Wintergill on the Hamer-Egton Bridge road. There is much new forestry here. Turn north along the road towards Egton for half a mile. One tempting track goes off earlier but it is the second and better one you want, turning backwards south-east at first but then curving round east. There are peat diggings, and quite a large pond to the right, but the track edges slightly north of east, keeping north of Pike Hill Moss, then east round the stream heads that go down into the short valley of Egton Grange. After 1½ miles from the Hamer-Egton road it turns north-east more or less along the ridge till in another mile it joins the Stape-Egton road. Keep north along this road for a hundred yards or so. A low bridge crosses a stream which drains the long curving bog below Murk Mire Moor, called 'Lady Bridge Slack'. As soon as you see hard going to the right, turn off south-east along a track which skirts this long bog along its eastern edge, then curves east and down to the Goathland-Egton road at Struntry Carr. Again you have to go 300 yards north towards Egton, when you will find a sign-posted track going off east through the woods and down to Murk Side. You cross a side stream, and then take the bridge across the Murk Esk, turning right along the far bank of the river into Beck Hole, where the Birch Hall Inn will welcome you. This is a very beautiful and sheltered stretch of the walk. It is also possible of course to get onto it from the Classic route at Hamer by going along the Egton road past Blue Wath to Wintergill.

At Beck Hole you have completed 34 miles by the shortest route and 40 by the longest. There are from 10 to 12 miles left to Ravenscar. Anyone needing accommodation at this point would need to go the extra 1¼ miles up the grassy old railway track to Goathland, but the Birch Hall Inn has food and a shop.

From Beck Hole there is a steep climb up to the railway

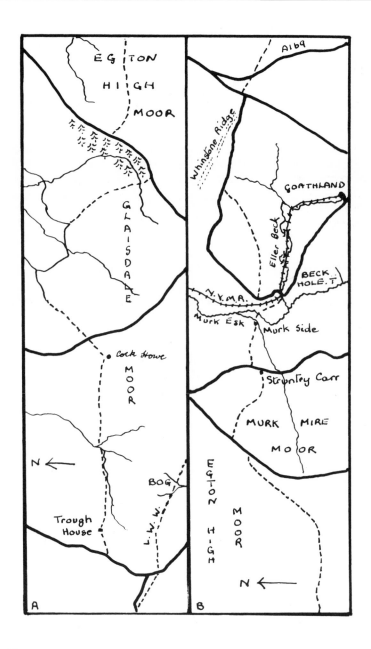

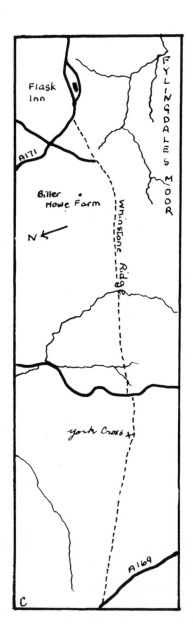

Flask
Inn

FYLINGDALES MOOR

A171

Biller
Howe Farm

N

Whinstone Ridge

York Cross †

A169

C

station. The road for Sil Howe and Whitby then goes due north. Almost immediately, from Hill House, a track goes off to the east towards Hawthorn Hill. There are several tracks here, and a Bronze Age 'settlement', but keeping to the northern edge of Hawthorn Hill fields you will strike a track heading north-east to the road again one mile West of Sil Howe.

Sil Howe is on the line of the Whinstone Ridge, a narrow outcrop of volcanic rock with stretches from the Tees via Great Ayton and Lonsdale. A broad track goes along it south-east for the next mile. You may keep to this track past Foster Howes and Ann's Cross to Lilla Cross and continue on the Classic route from there. A more varied route is to turn off this track 1½ miles from Sil Howe for York Cross (the stump of a cross set in a socket). The path from here is not definitive but is permitted, being largely through Forestry Commission land. In planting it the Commission kindly left a route through by Pike Hill to Blea Hill Howe, though part of this is on Forestry tracks.

From Blea Hill in reasonable conditions you can see the Flask Inn on the Whitby-Scarborough road almost due east, and due east is your route down Biller Howe Turf Rigg keeping to the right-hand or south side of Biller Howe Nook Slack, a marshy stream. This brings you out at Billera Cottage. From here the lane past Pond Farm to the main road can be followed, or it is possible to take a short cut up the ridge in front of the cottage and along a stone wall direct towards the Flask, with just a field to cross (not definitive). N.B. The track past Biller Howe Farm is not a public right-of-way and should be avoided.

From the Flask Inn there is one mile of main road towards Scarborough before you meet the Classic route coming in on the right over Jugger Howe. Here you take the well-worn path up the embankment to your left and head over Stony Marl Moor to the Beacon. If you wish to finish in style at the bar of the Raven Hall Hotel the pleasantest way is to cross the road beyond the Beacon, go along the stone wall and down a steep bit of moor to another lane 'Robin Hood Road', where the Ben Hingston seat has been placed. A footpath goes on, skirting the top of the old alum works and coming right out at the Information Centre and hotel entrance.

Note: During the shooting season, i.e. after August 12, the alternative routes beyond Rosedale should be avoided. The Classic route, which goes along the boundary between the shoots, is generally the safest and most acceptable then.

Suggested Alternative Walks

(suitable for larger parties or for sponsoring)

I should not be writing this chapter because I don't approve of large parties! Sometimes a school or firm may wish to go out together *en masse*, but those who wish to bring hundreds together to raise money for some charitable purpose should do it in a sports stadium, or arrange something useful like litter-collection or tree-planting. Walking should be left to small parties who organise themselves.

Wherever a particular challenge walk is likely to attract large numbers, and probably large parties, it is now clear that certain criteria should be followed. (1) Farms and villages should be avoided or by-passed as far as possible, particularly at 'unsociable hours'. (2) The route should follow hard ground, and avoid soft peats liable to erosion. (3) The route should be easy to follow, preferably sign-posted in advance. (4) There should be adequate support and rescue points with easy access. (5) A circular route is preferable so that heavy transport can stay in one place, avoiding expense and inconvenience to others. However, a straight route sometimes has special historical interest, in which case the availability of public transport and accommodation at each end is desirable.

SUGGESTED WALKS

1. The Drover's Road, or Hambleton Drove Road.

This ancient high-level track from Sutton Bank to Scarth Nick over Black Hambleton is 3 miles of minor road and 8 miles of firm grassy lane, with magnificent views. For a sponsored challenge why not do it there and back, 22 miles?

2. The Monk's Trod.

This is an interesting variation on the previous walk, starting at Byland Abbey and following the old monk's footpath to Rievaulx, then on by Caydale Mill and Murton Grange to re-join the Drove Road for Scarth Nick, a route used by Rievaulx monks to visit their granges at Welbury and elsewhere. Distance 20 miles (to Scarth Nick).

1½ miles from Byland Abbey, beyond the steep part of Wass Bank, leave the road through a forest gate left. Very soon take the right-hand fork through the plantation, coming out on the Thirsk-Helmsley road opposite a lodge. Fifty yards to the east of the lodge is a large double gate leading to new farm buildings. The Monks' Trod is easy to follow almost straight north along Claythwaite Rigg, passing to the east of the buildings. It comes down to the Scawton-Rievaulx road at Ashberry Farm. A footpath continues behind the farm and through the woods on the true right bank of the Rye to Tile House, marked here and there by ancient trees. An alternative from Ashberry is to take the lane past Rievaulx Abbey itself. Half way up the village another farm lane turns left to Bow Bridge. From here instead of taking the Tile House footpath you can follow the lane to Old Byland, where the Byland Abbey monks first settled, and thence to Caydale Mill. From Tile House the path goes through a forestry plantation up the valley to the mill.

Just past Murton Grange, you meet the road that goes down to Hawnby. Directly opposite is a gate and a forestry track leading through Peak Scar Wood. Keep round this track to the other side of the valley and climb up the ridge – Noddle End – to a barn on top. From here (the path goes south and west of the barn) a good track goes west along the ridge with Gowerdale to the north, and comes out on the Drove Road opposite the High Paradise Farm gate. (Good accommodation there). Eight miles north along the Drove Road is Scarth Nick.

3. The Shepherd's Round.

This is a much more ambitious walk of 40 miles, first suggested by Alan Neasham of Osmotherley, and almost as strenuous as the Lyke Wake Walk, but keeping to firmer ground. A schedule of 18 hours and a 4.00 am start are indicated. Start (appropriately) at the Sheepwash above Osmotherley and follow the Lyke Wake route as far as Bloworth Crossing (support point after 10 miles at Clay

Bank). From Bloworth turn south down Rudland Rigg. In just over a mile you reach the Cammon Stone (probably 'Celtic', but it has a later inscription in Hebrew on it). Just over half a mile past that a footpath comes up on the left from Spout House in Farndale and down on the right to Cockayne and Cow Sike in Bransdale. A few hundred yards further on is a bridle path going down in the same direction – either of those will do. From Cockayne keep right along the road that goes down the west side of Bransdale. After 2½ miles you turn right at Bonfield Gill by the track across Bilsdale East Moor to Crossets and Fangdale Beck in Farndale. (The footpath goes round High Crossets to the north). If thought necessary, support could come up into Bransdale from Helmsley via Carlton and Cow House Bank (narrow road) but otherwise Fangdale Beck lane end would do (12 miles from Clay Bank). There is a shop in the Post Office at Fangdale Beck (the path goes past the shop door) and the Sun Inn at Spout House, with its 15th century cruck house now restored, is ¾ mile south on the main Helmsley road.

From the Post office the lane goes up the little village and turns left towards Malkin Bower Farm (refreshments). After a hundred yards a footpath turns right – a muddy lane also turns right at Malkin Bower – for an old quarry and cairns on the moor edge. The track then keeps west or south of west, to the south of the ruins of Wether House, as far as Honey Hill, also ruined. From there a better track goes south-west to the Ryedale road and then south into Hawnby (Inn). The 8 mile stretch from Fangdale Beck is through an area very important to the shepherd-monks of Rievaulx Abbey – Wether Cote, Ewe Cote, Gimmer Cote and Woolhouse Croft near Laskill were all part of their sheep rearing enterprise. It was they who brought improved agriculture to Bilsdale and they would often use the route through Bransdale to reach their other granges such as Esklets.

From Hawnby take the road for Kepwick past New Hall and south of Arden Hall. A rough lane up a steep hill brings you to the Drove Road again at Kepwick Bank top (4 miles). Six miles north along the Drove Road over Black Hambleton will bring you back to the Sheepwash.

This is a magnificent walk with a considerable amount of climbing on it, and it should not be undertaken lightly. A shorter alternative, or 'Short Round', would be to turn off the Lyke Wake route at Carlton Bank and south to Cock Howe and all the way down Bilsdale West Moor past High Thwaites and Low Thwaites into Hawnby – then back as above, about 25 miles. Taken as a challenge walk, the Shepherd's Round should be done in 18 hours. But it is a fine two-day walk with accommodation in Fangdale Beck, Bilsdale or Hawnby. A leaflet is available from the Lyke Wake Club (25p + s.a.e.) also badge (£1 + s.a.e.)

4. The Rail Trail

This is a very different walk, 20-26 miles according to route, involves using British Rail to get back from finishing point to starting point, and British Rail may be used to get to the starting point. Half the route then lies on the cinder track of the remarkable Rosedale Ironstone Railway whose history is given briefly in the Lyke Wake Walk pages.

When I was a boy in Middlesbrough much of our walking was done by using the Eskdale railway. Fortunately that is still possible and much more use should be made of it. In reconnaissance for the ski-crossing in 1963, when most roads were blocked, the railway was invaluable. The first trains leave Middlesbrough at 5.26 and 7.23 so it is possible to start walking in Battersby by at least 8.0 a.m. The last train (winter) leaves Glaisdale at 7.49 p.m., Lealholme and Danby at some five minute intervals after that.

From Battersby station you take the road to Ingleby Greenhowe for ¼ mile, then turn left on the lane to Bank Foot and Turkey Nab. At Bank Foot turn right along the track of the old ironstone railway which goes along the foot of Turkey Nab. (Turkey is a corruption of 'Thorkill'). After two miles, just past some cottages, you begin the long climb up the incline down which the tubs of iron ore used to run. The line is followed (see Lyke Wake Walk details) right through to the Lion Inn at Blakey, or further on into Rosedale itself, even as far as the old West Rosedale mine and into Rosedale itself, and the Abbey. Indeed, if train times have been checked, it might be possible to go on by Low Hamer, Leaf Howe, Keldy and Cawthorne to Pickering, and take the North York Moors Railway all the way back via Grosmont to Battersby. But otherwise the point of return to aim for (either from the Lion or from Rosedale) is Red House and Dale Head farms from which the George Gap Causeway leads over into Fryupdale. Follow this right down to Fryup Hall and go by Fairy Cross Plain, Stonebeck Farm and Crossley Side to Ainthorpe and Danby station. The alternative would be to take the Trough House track as described in the 'Lyke Wake Way' pages, and go along Glaisdale Rigg to Glaisdale Station, or to Lealholme. Again this is a highly recommended walk with special interest to railway enthusiasts.

(The George Gap Causeway is now perhaps the best stretch of flagged causeway left on the high moors, since the one over Urra Moor has been destroyed by a firebreak. Anyone wanting to sponsor something really useful and worthwhile should consider the cleaning and reclamation of this ancient causeway.)

VERSE BY THE CHIEF DIRGER

Storm Longing

Come, friends o' my heart, to the hills we'll fly,
    Where the high winds never rest,
But storm and cry on the Riggs that lie
    To the eastward crest on crest;
Where rain and sleet in tempest beat
    Round many an ancient Cross,
From Crookstaff Hill to Wheeldale Gill,
    From Bloworth to Yarsley Moss.
When the sea-roke spread on Botton Head
    Rolls down to the dale beneath,
And our way we thread with careful tread
    Through the gloom of the trackless heath;
When the sea-wind snarls from Stony Marls
    And the sky's a leaden cloud
That hides the brow of Shunner Howe
    Like a Norseman's funeral shroud.
But what reck we of roke or storm
    Or the furies overhead?
A song we'll sing as on we swing
    With sure and steady tread.
Though boggets growl and ratchets howl
    As we tramp on side by side,
Through the night that's black with storm and wrack
    Our steps the gods shall guide.

(1935)

69

Transportation and Accommodation

THERE are buses from Northallerton to Osmotherley, from Stokesley to Helmsley (Fridays, Saturdays only) from Scarborough to Middlesbrough past the Falcon and Flask Inns, and from Ravenscar to Scarborough (not Sundays) but it is best to ring United Services Darlington 468771 or Whitby 602146 for latest information. Returning by public transport from Ravenscar to Osmotherley can take longer than walking back – make it a double!

For accommodation too it is best to get the latest list from National Park Office, Helmsley 70657. However, a few reliable places are – Queen Catherine (the Club's HQ), Osmotherley 209. Ravenscar (0723): Mrs. Greenfield, Smugglers' Rock, 87004; Mrs. Pilley, Crag Hill 870925; Mrs Pease, Ness Hall, 870536; Camping and Bunk House, Mr. White, Bent Rigg 870475. Village Hall is available for large parties - inquire Mrs. Russell, Ravenhurst, Church Road, 870801.

For Lyke Wake Way, Shepherds' Round:- Bilsdale (04396); Beacon Guest 320; Fangdale Grange 353; Mrs Wood, Ewe Cote 255; Wether Cote 260; Hawnby Hotel 249 Goathland (0947); Whitfield House 86215; Barnet House 86201; Beckhole 86428; Glaisdale - Egton Banks Farm 87289; Anglers Rest 87261.

Some travel reports by Ben Hingston, who had no car, but always managed to get from Northallerton to start his 212 crossings, and usually managed to get home to Northallerton when he finished: 11th April 1982: Cold north wind; frost till 10. Light sleet, and a brief hailstorm at noon. Left YHA 6.30, Shooting Hut 7.15, Cock Howe 8.15, Botton Head 9.35. Icicles in railway culverts – Wheeldale Stepping Stones 15.00; met Gerald Orchard on Simon Howe. Burn Howe 17.20; lingered among Helwath daffodils for beer and grub. Windmill 19.03 – Gerald waiting, lift to York for

21.05 train.

24th April 1982: First bus to Osmotherley. Start 7.00 (same route – Ben had his own favourite variations), finish 19.30. Lift to Scarborough, bus to York, train home.

9th August 1982: First bus, Classic route. Found weary and lame man a mile from Beacon Howe and helped him to finish, thereby getting a lift to York.

14th January 1983: (200th crossing): Left Osmotherley 21.35. Slept in Swainby Shooting Hut for an hour. Moor filthy with pools of meltwater. Cloud high; clear; constant visual delights. At Ravenscar a passing car whisked me into Scarborough to catch the 5 o'clock train and I was home at 7.30. Slept soundly.

Conditions for Challenge Walk

1. The Walk is the complete traverse of the North York Moors along the main West – East watershed within 24 hours.

2. Start from Eastern end of Osmotherley Reservoir (Lyke Wake Stone) (Grid Ref. SE 469994). Finish at Beacon Howe, Ravenscar (Grid. Ref. NZ 970013). For record attempts (prior notification necessary), from Triangulation Pillar 982 on Scarth Wood Moor, Grid. Ref. 459997, to bar of Raven Hall Hotel (closed in winter). Food and accommodation cannot be relied on in Ravenscar unless ordered in advance.

3. Route must cross Stokesley-Helmsley road between Clay Bank and Orterley lane end; the Whitby-Pickering road between Sil Howe and Saltersgate; the Whitby-Scarborough road between Evan Howe and the Falcon Inn. Route must stick to the tops as far as possible.

4. Before doing the walk send a stamped addressed envelope to the Lyke Wake Club, Goulton Grange, Swainby, Northallerton, DL6 3HP for a leaflet with latest information.

5. A report of the walk with details of route and times should be sent to the same address with s.a.e. and 20p per head for Card of Completion (and Condolence). Please do not telephone or call. Leaflet includes list of badges, ties, etc, available.

6. Please take care to keep the moors tidy. Carry away any litter you bring with you. Collect and bury any you find. Do not smoke near heather. Do not disturb anyone at unreasonable hours.

NOTES

1. Total amount of climbing on the Classic route is 5,000 ft.
2. A ski-crossing in 24 hours daylight will be accepted.

SUPPORT PARTY LOCATIONS

Location	Map Ref.	Time Schedule 16 hour walk
Sheepwash Car Park (start)	SE 469 994	0000
Clay Bank Car Park	NZ 573 035	0230 - 0300
Ralph Cross	NZ 676 019	0600 - 0630
Hamer (500 yards North of Hamer House)	SE 744 995	0830 - 0900
Eller Beck Bridge	SE 857 983	1130 - 1200
Jugger Howe slip road	NZ 945 003	1500 - 1530
Beacon Howes (finish)	NZ 970 013	1600